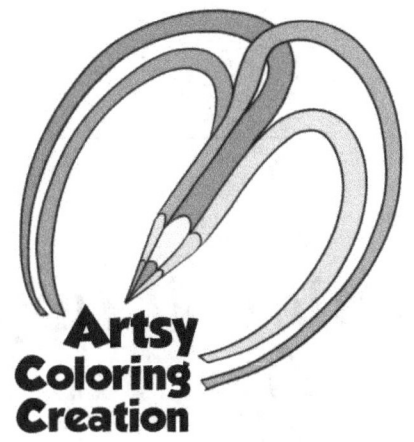

Artsy Coloring Creation

A Coloring Adventure
UNDERWATER

A coloring book featuring 36 exclusive unique hand drawn scenes from what is in the water. Discover the different marine sea life and the mysteries of the deep dark ocean.

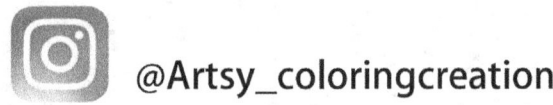

@Artsy_coloringcreation

This Book Belongs to:

_____

A little coloring adventure
Underwater

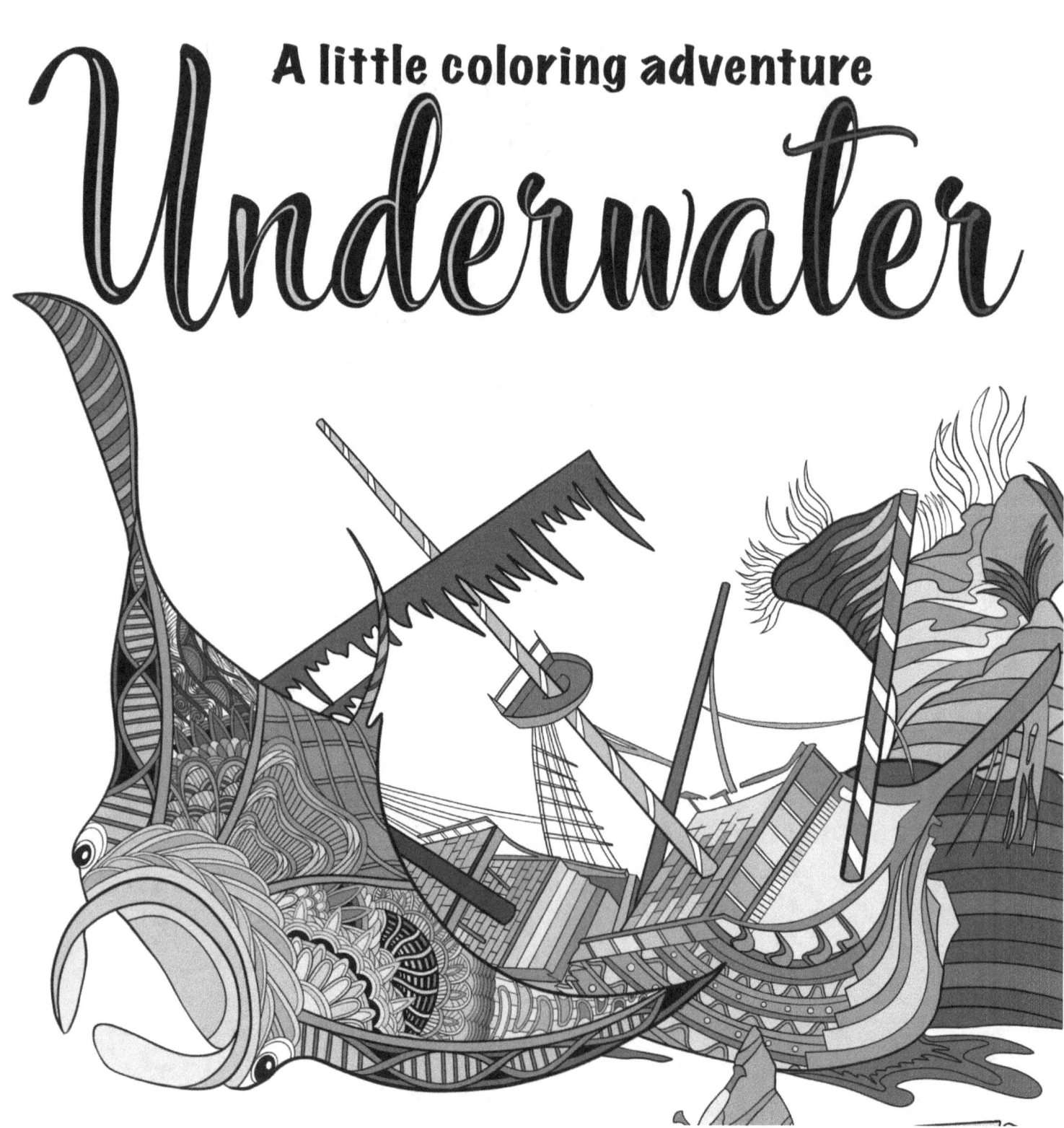

About the Creator

Hi, I am Matthew Pang. I am an amateur photographer and loves sketching and landscape drawing. I enjoyed landscape sketching during my youth years and have been practising during my free time.

About Underwater

Join the adventure of exploring the underwater world. The journey that brings you from the koi fishes in the water fountain ponds, to turtles in the coral reefs, the great white shark in the deep sea and all the way to the mythological sea serpent that lies in the deep dark ocean and the mythological lost city of Atlantis.

THE STORY...

7 scenes from the underwater world will transport you into the world of marine life. Take a dive and explore them. The ponds that you will typically have in your backyard.

The lakes that consist of fresh and salt water fishes. Moving on to the fast flowing streams of river, will you survive the coloring of the Piranhas? Or will you move on.... To the Coral bay where you can imagine the colorful reefs and turtles in the sunny turquoise waters.

Then, as you move further, you'll be trapped in the open sea. Now we dive deep into explore what is ever more mysterious with the mythological tales.. Will you find the serpent? You will about to find out !

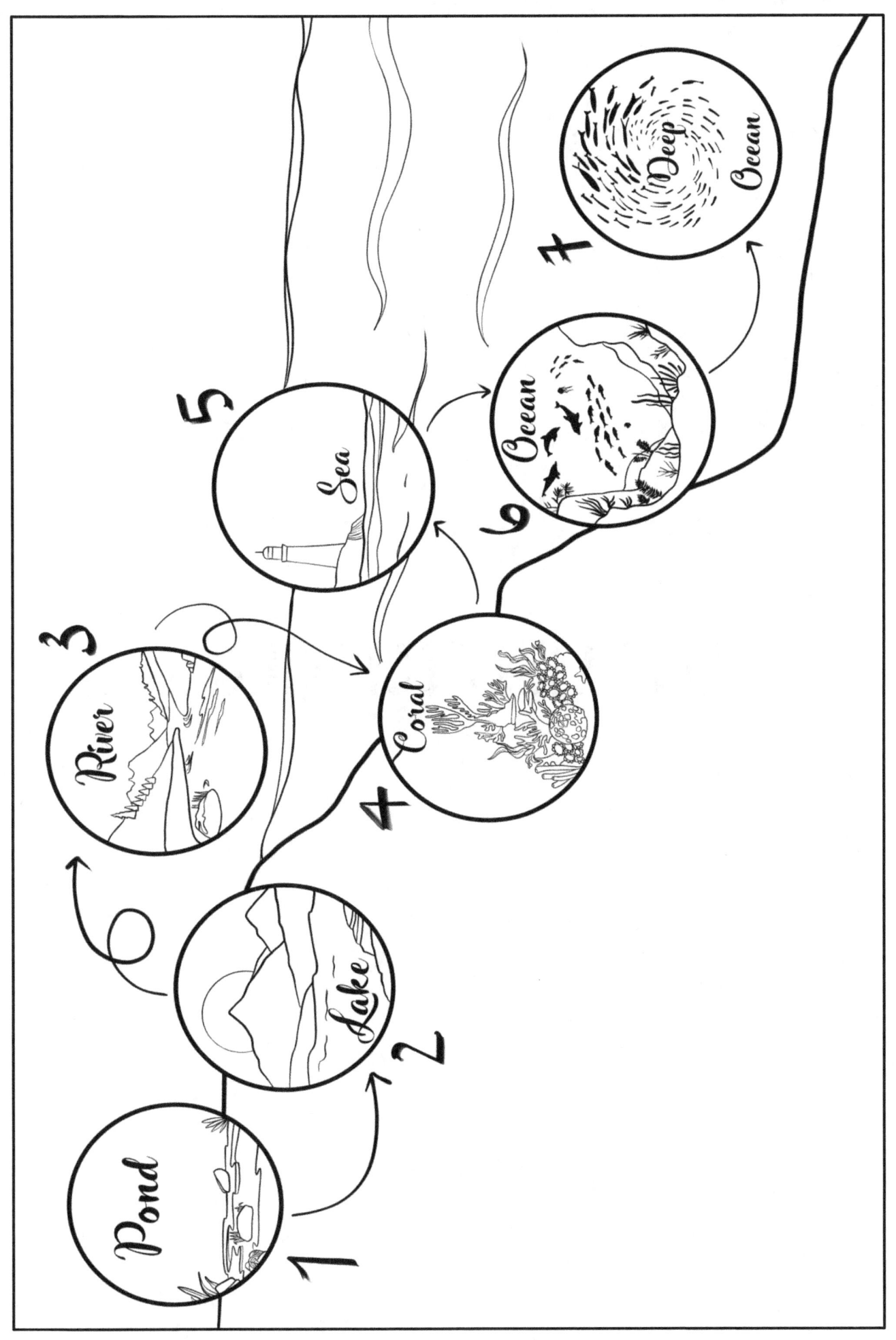

LETS START COLORING...

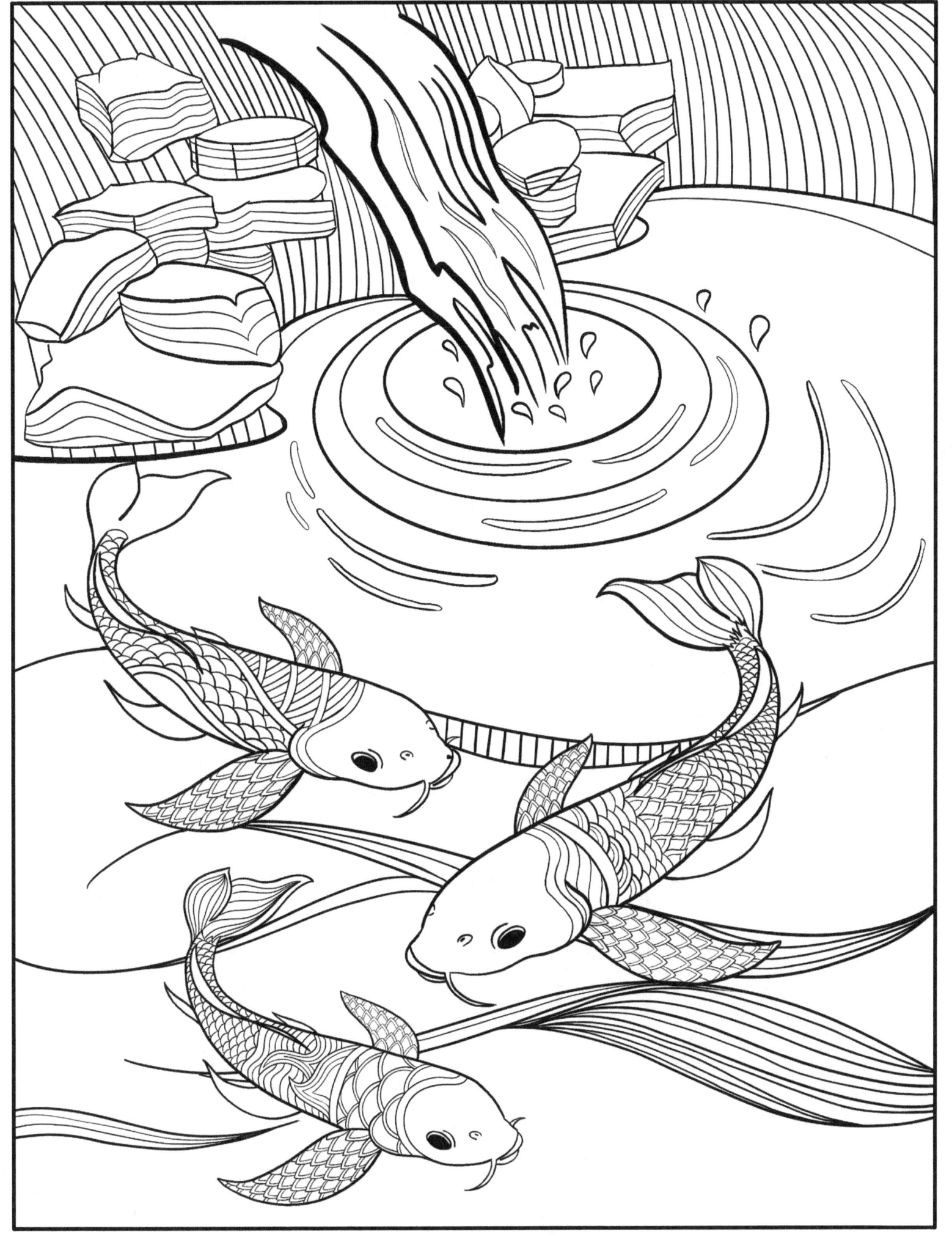

Pond
Koi

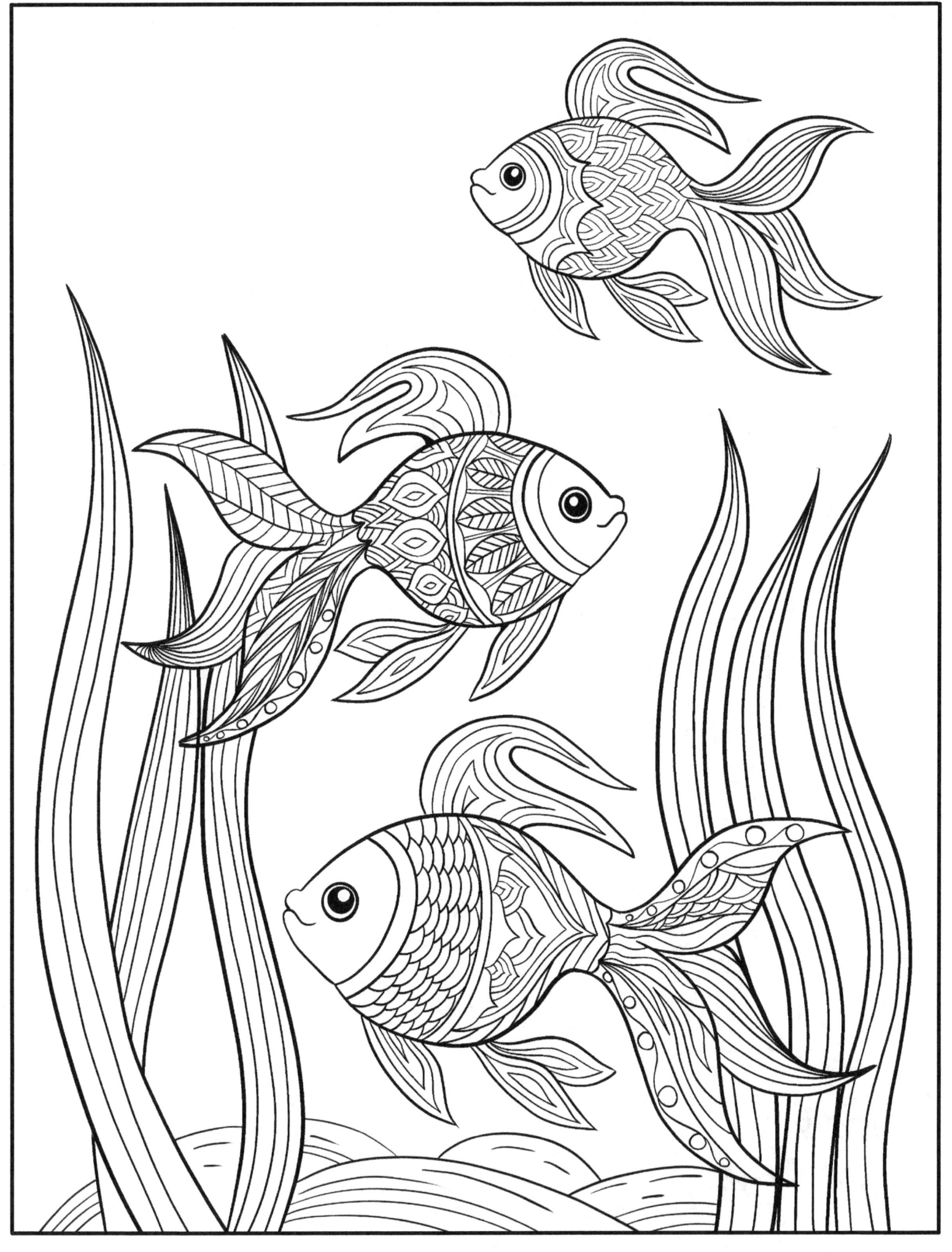

Pond
Gold Fish

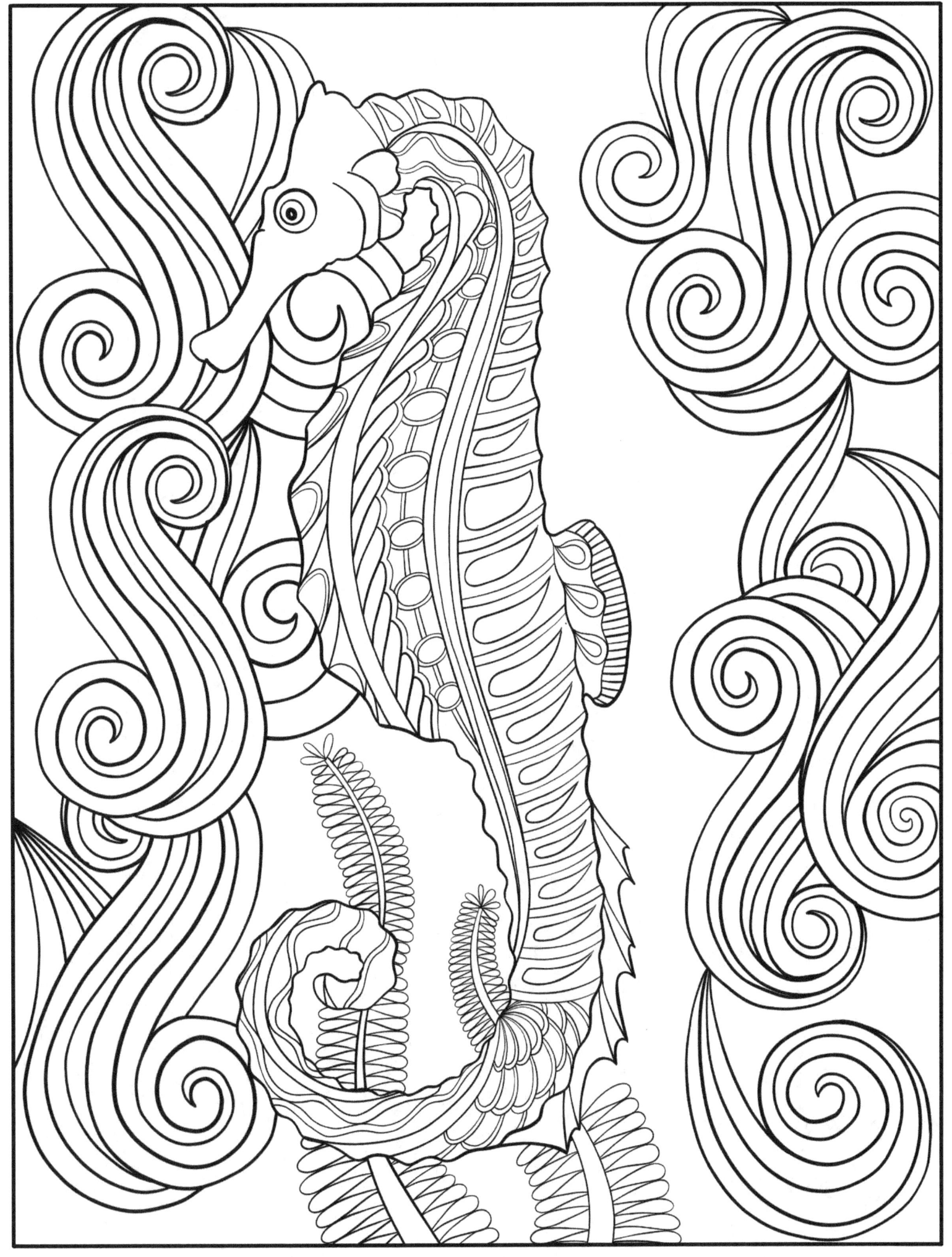

Pond Seahorse

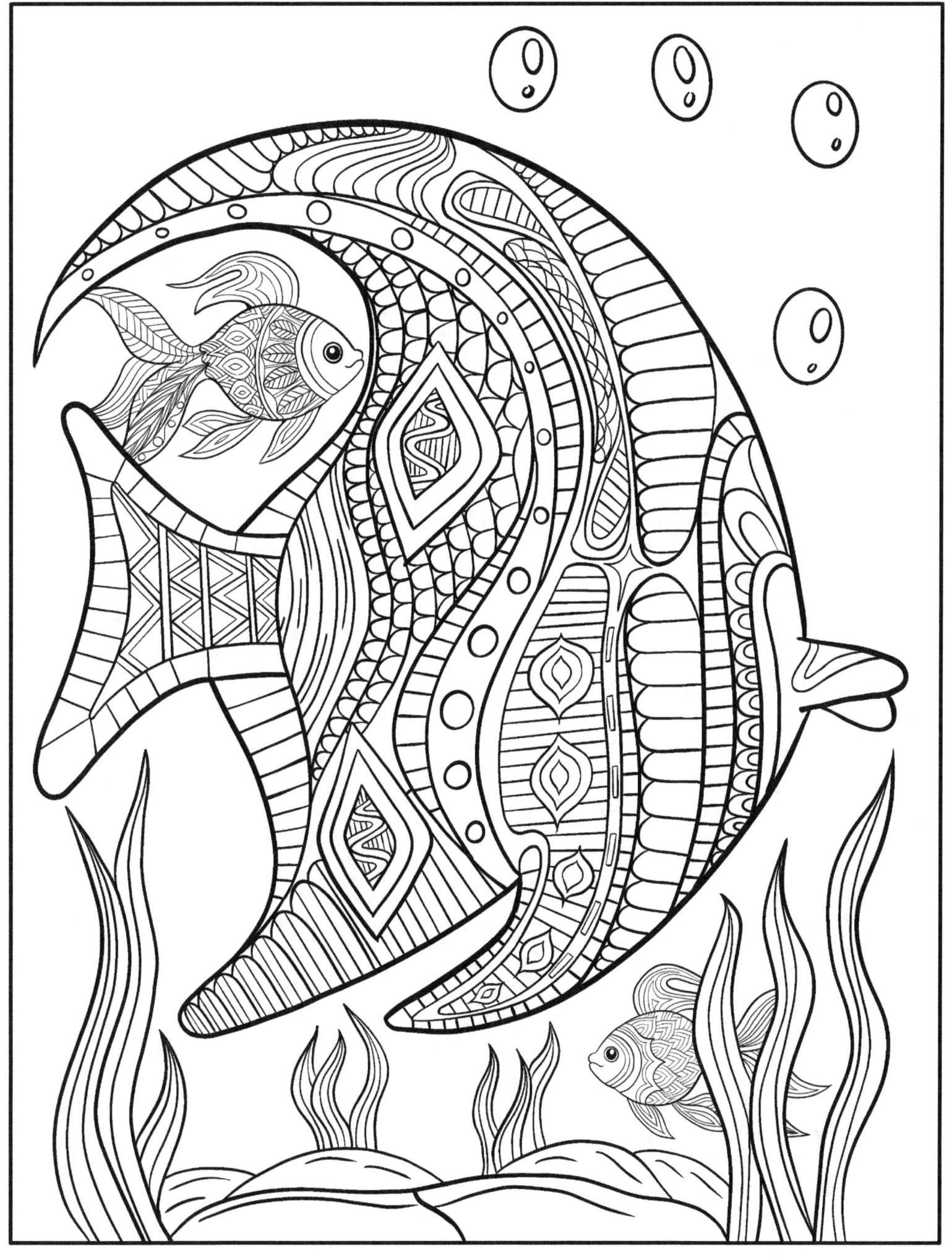

Pond
Angel Fish

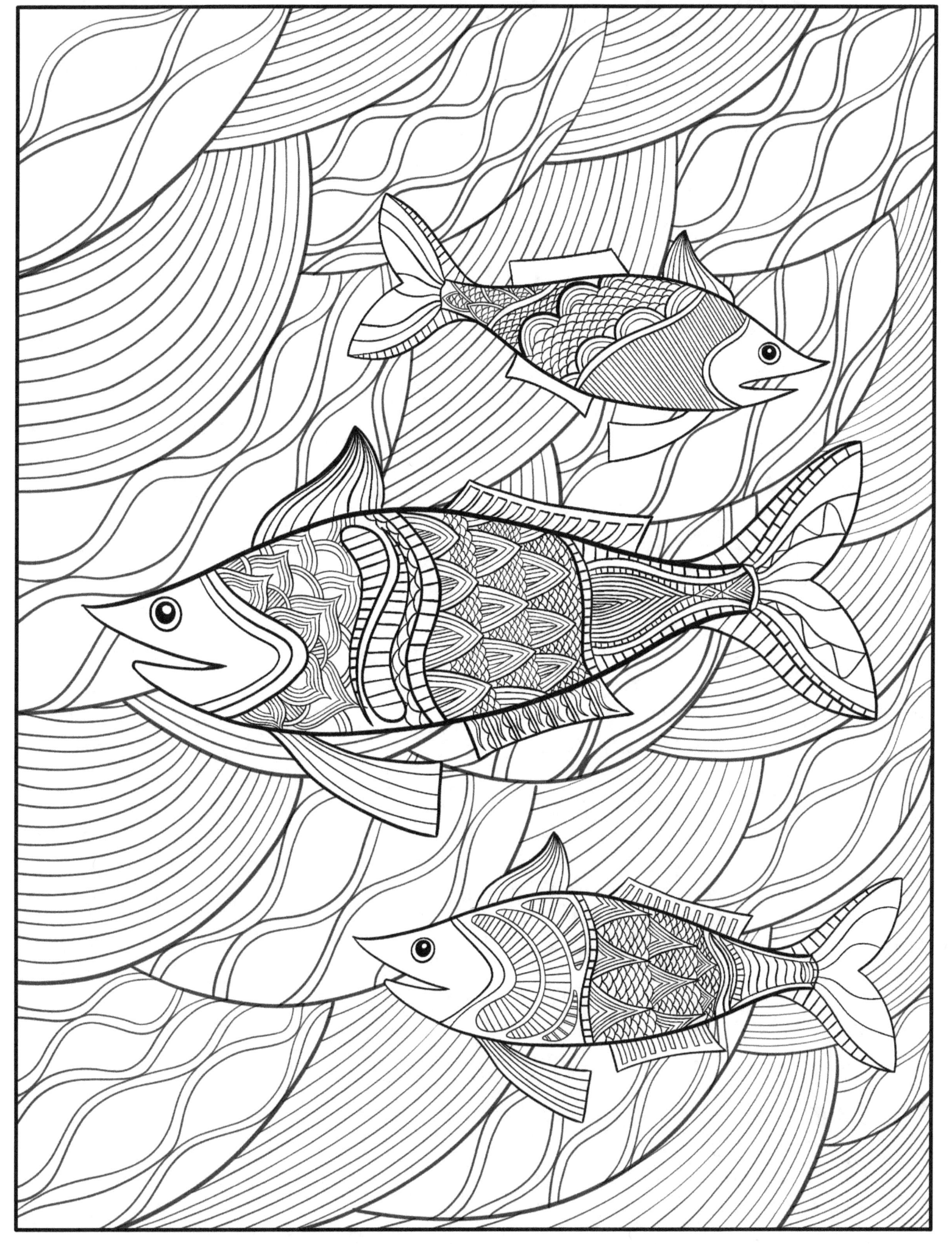

Lake Mackerel

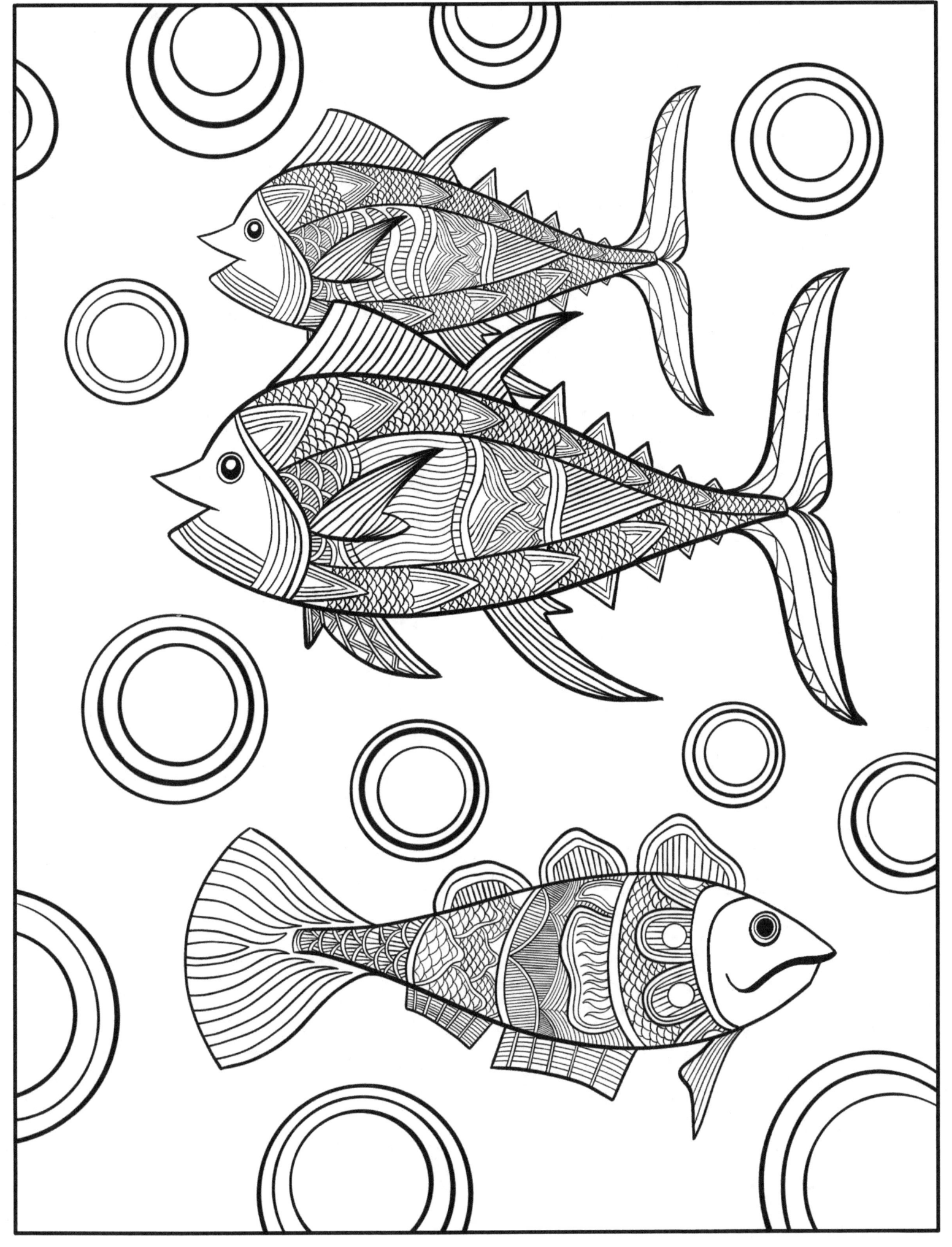

Lake
Tuna

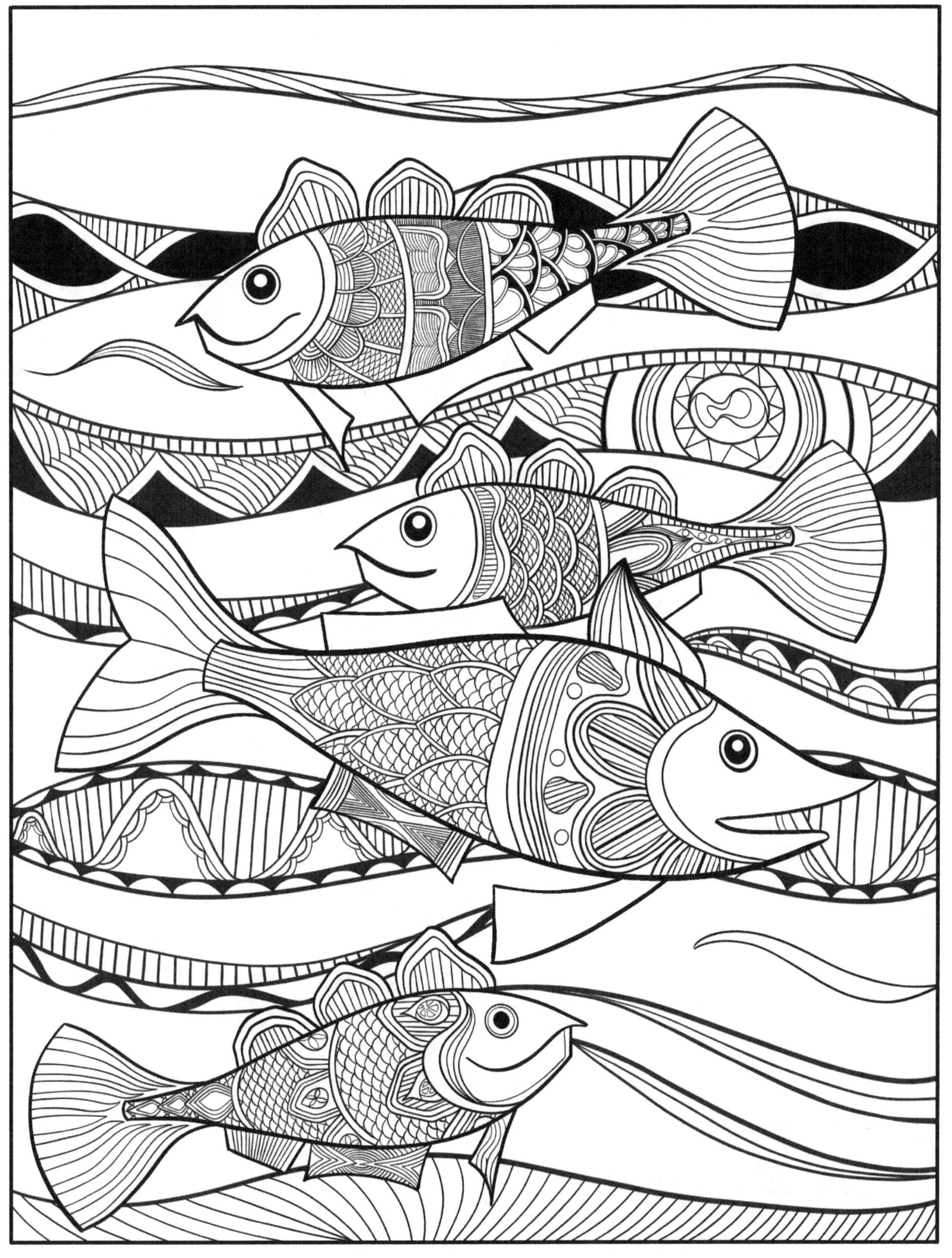

Lake
Cod & Mackerel

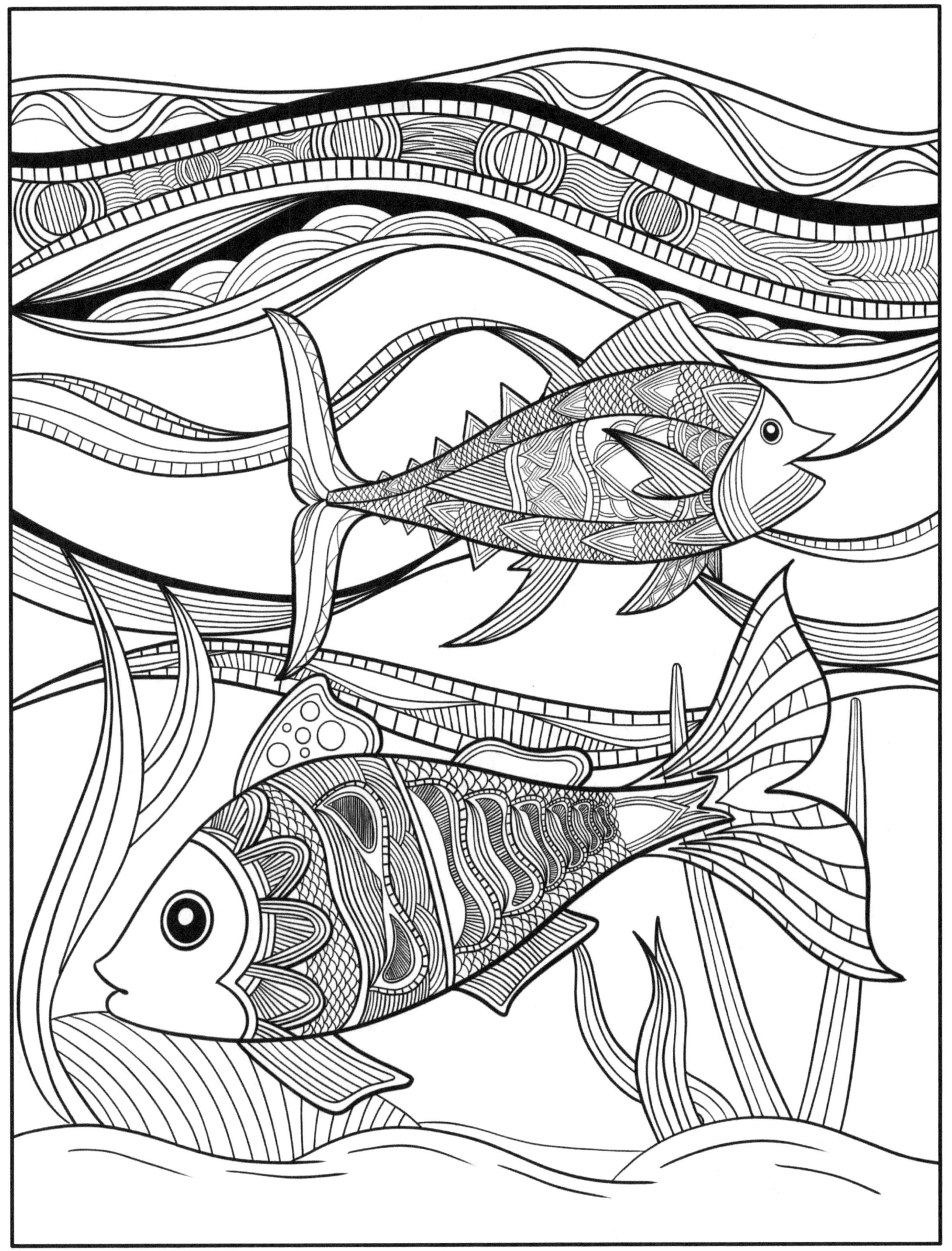

Lake Surmullets

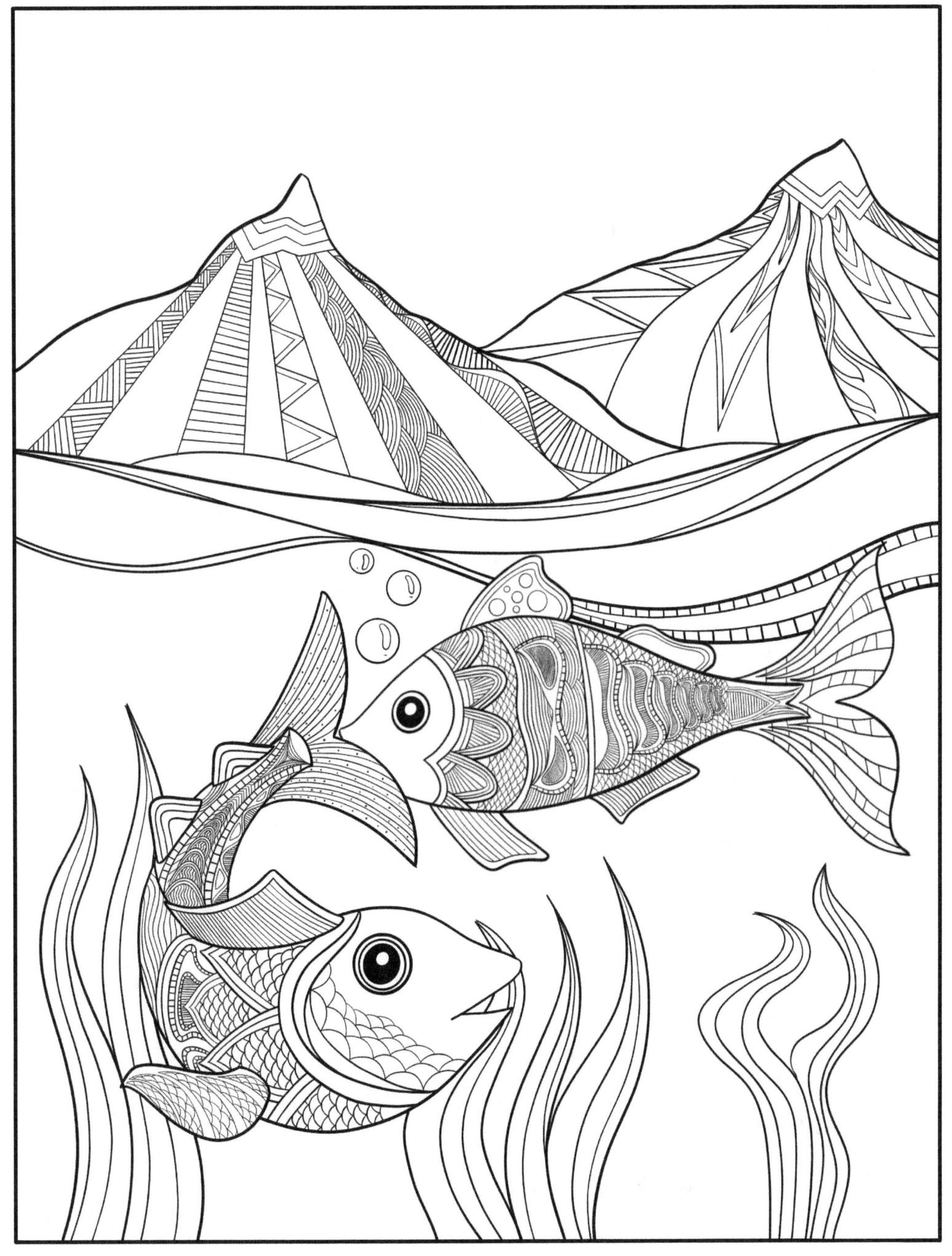

Lake
Rocky mountains

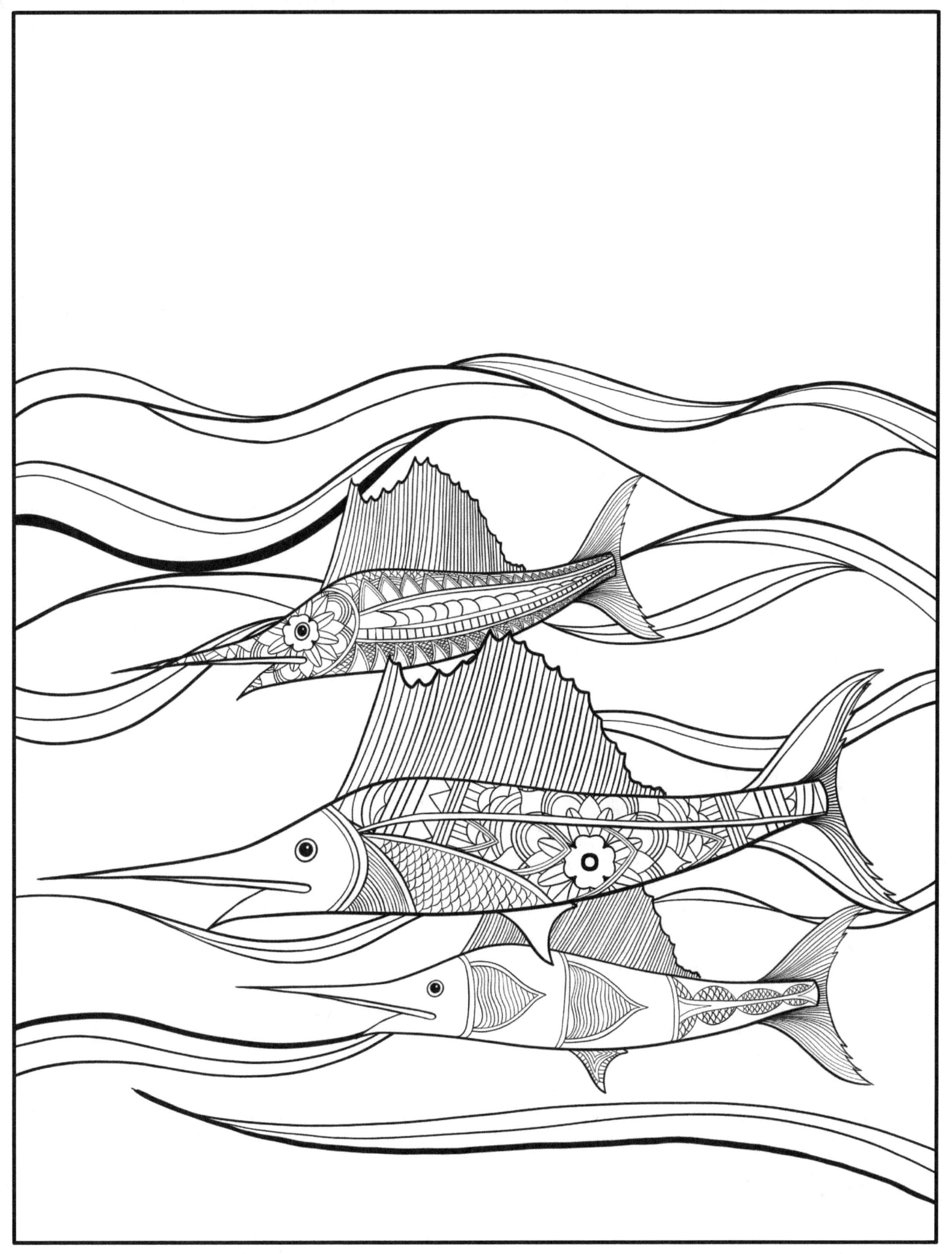

Lake
Sail Fish

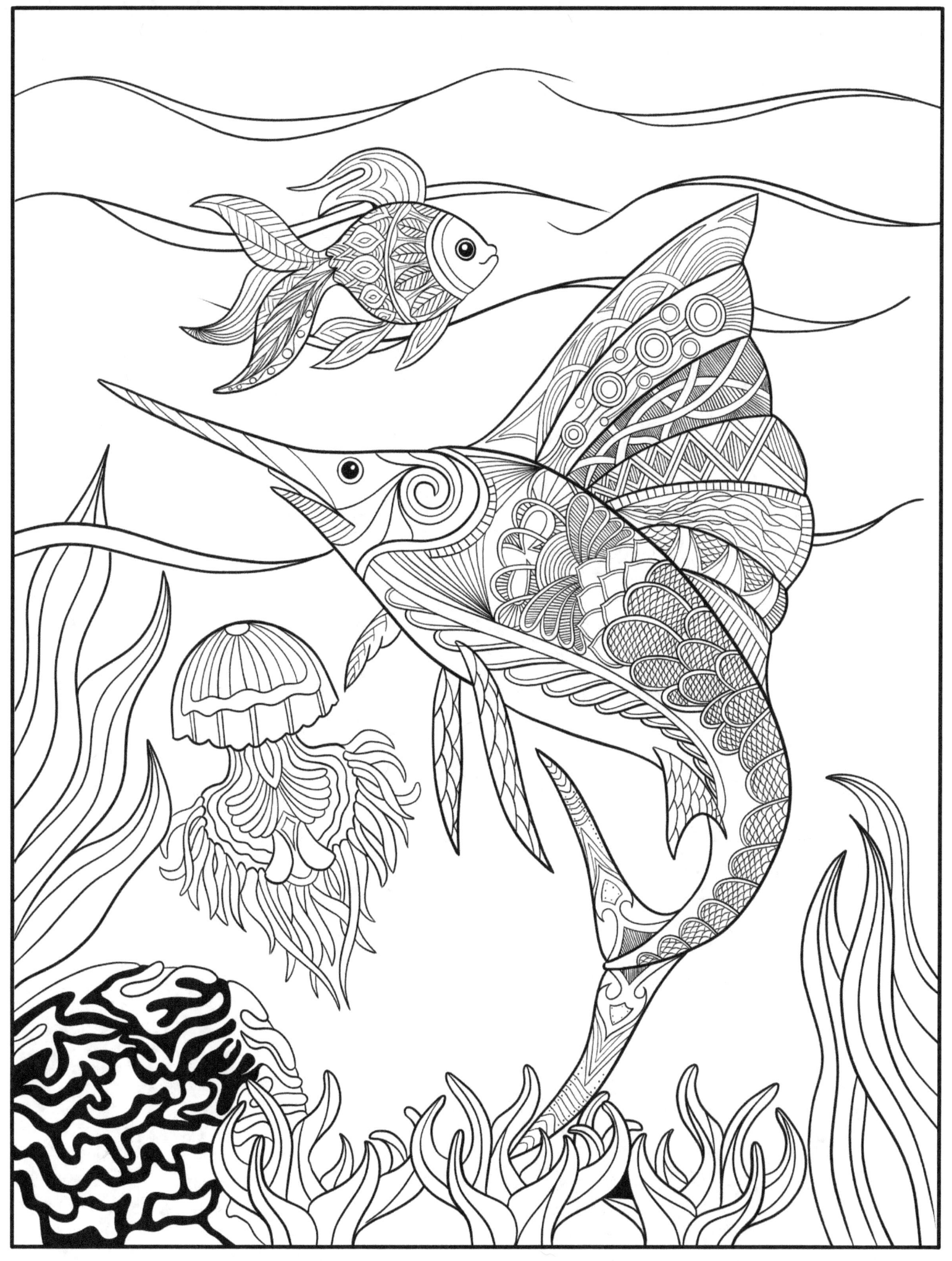

Lake

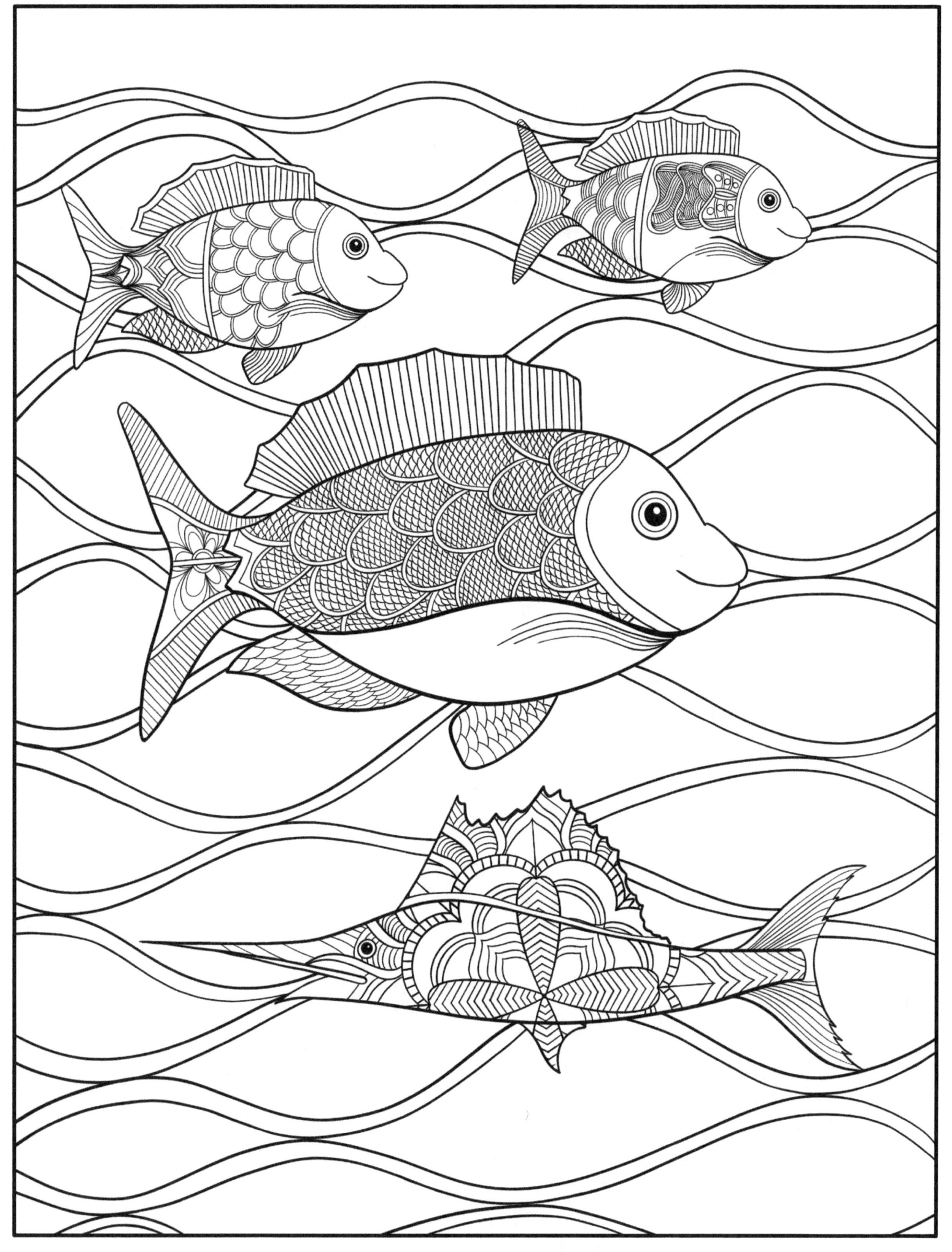

Lake

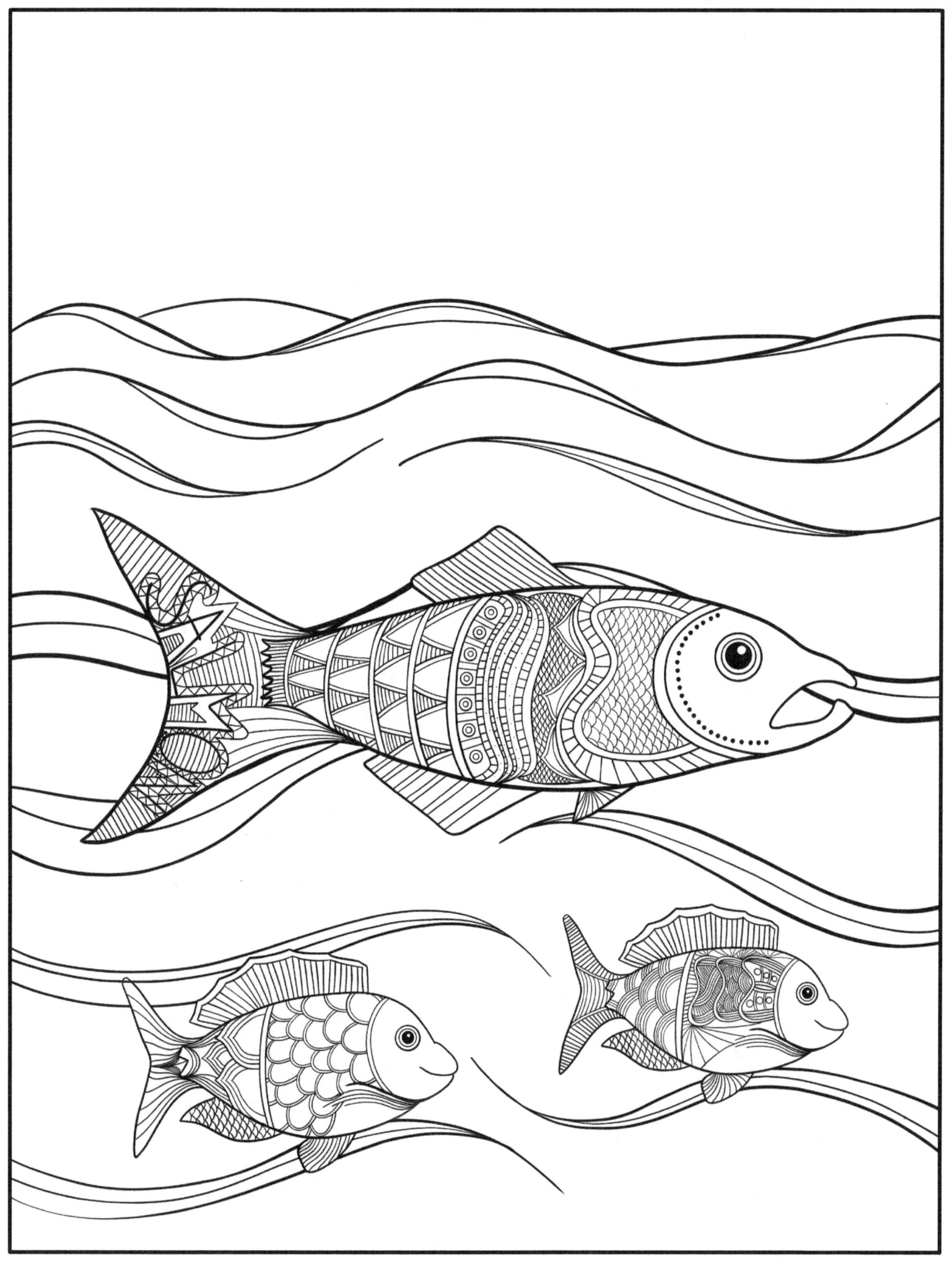

River Salmon

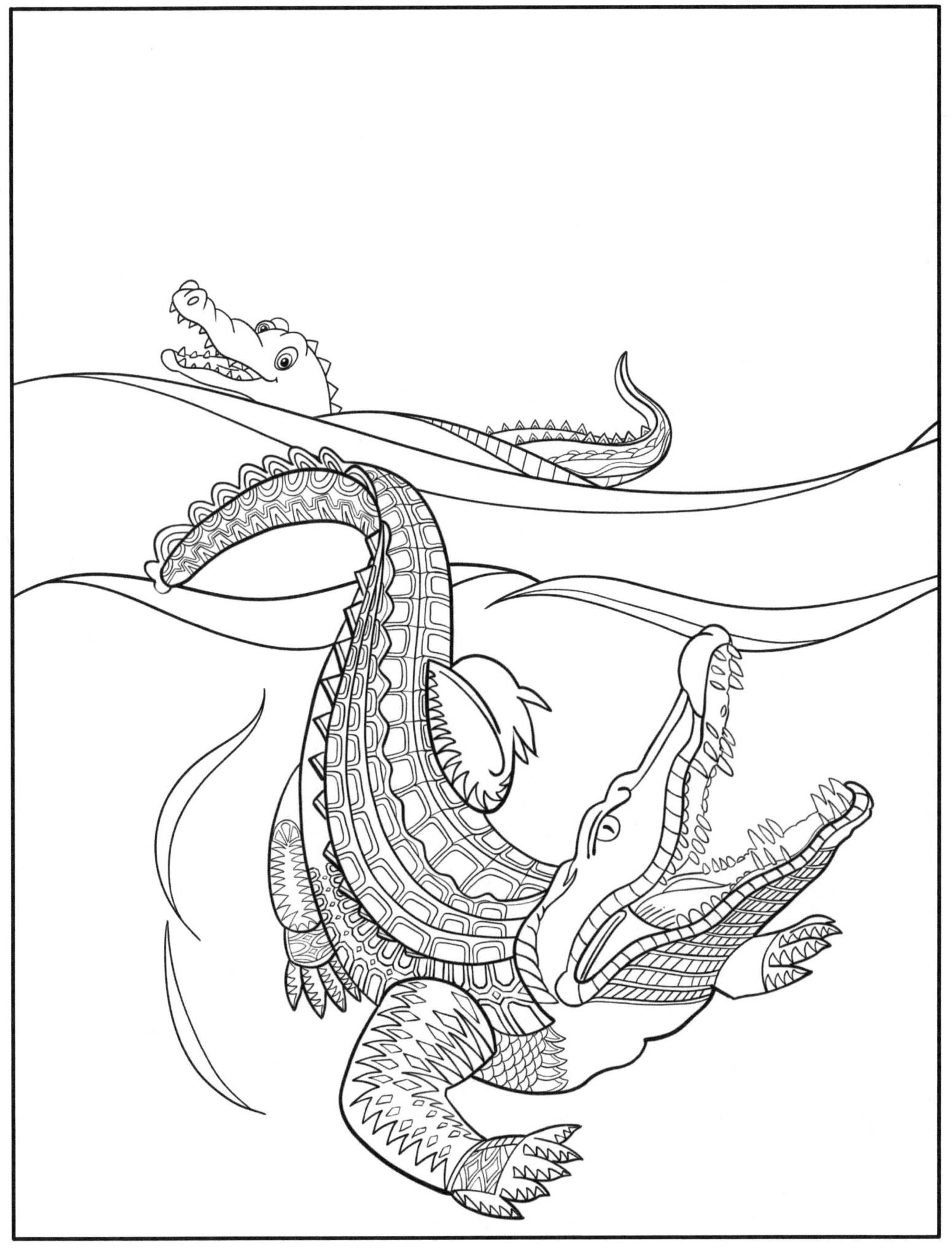

Lake Crocodile

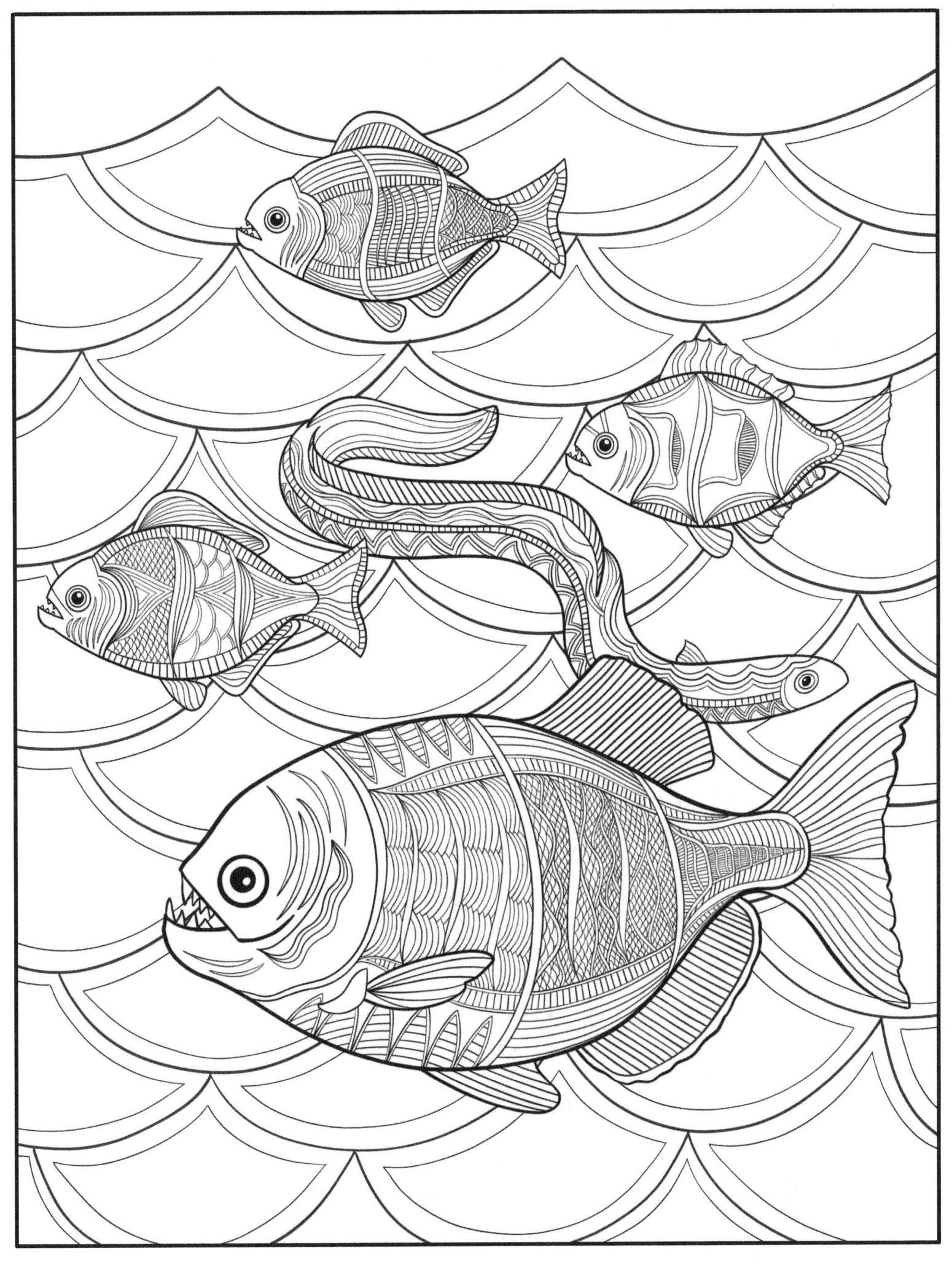

River
Piranha

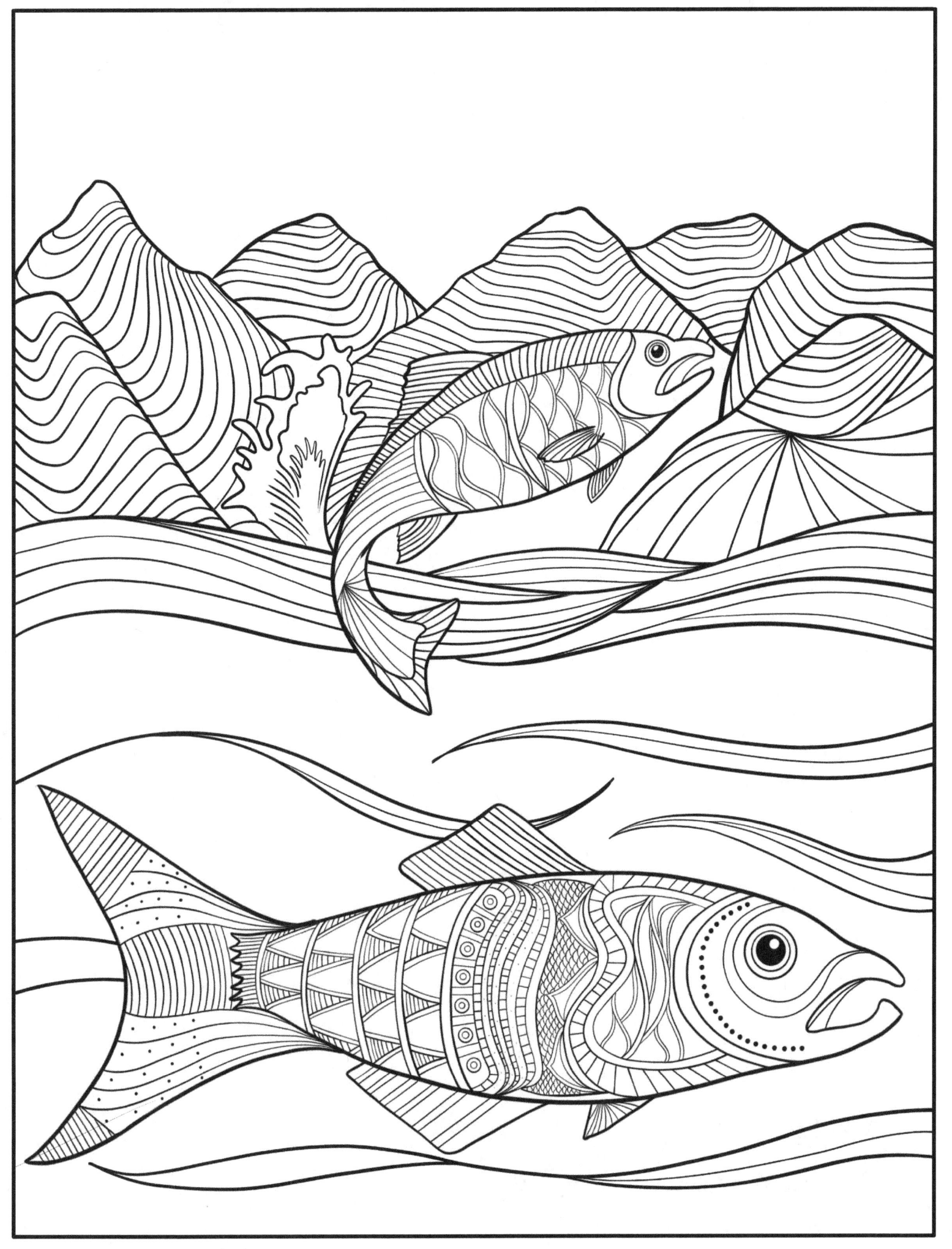

River
Salmon along mountains

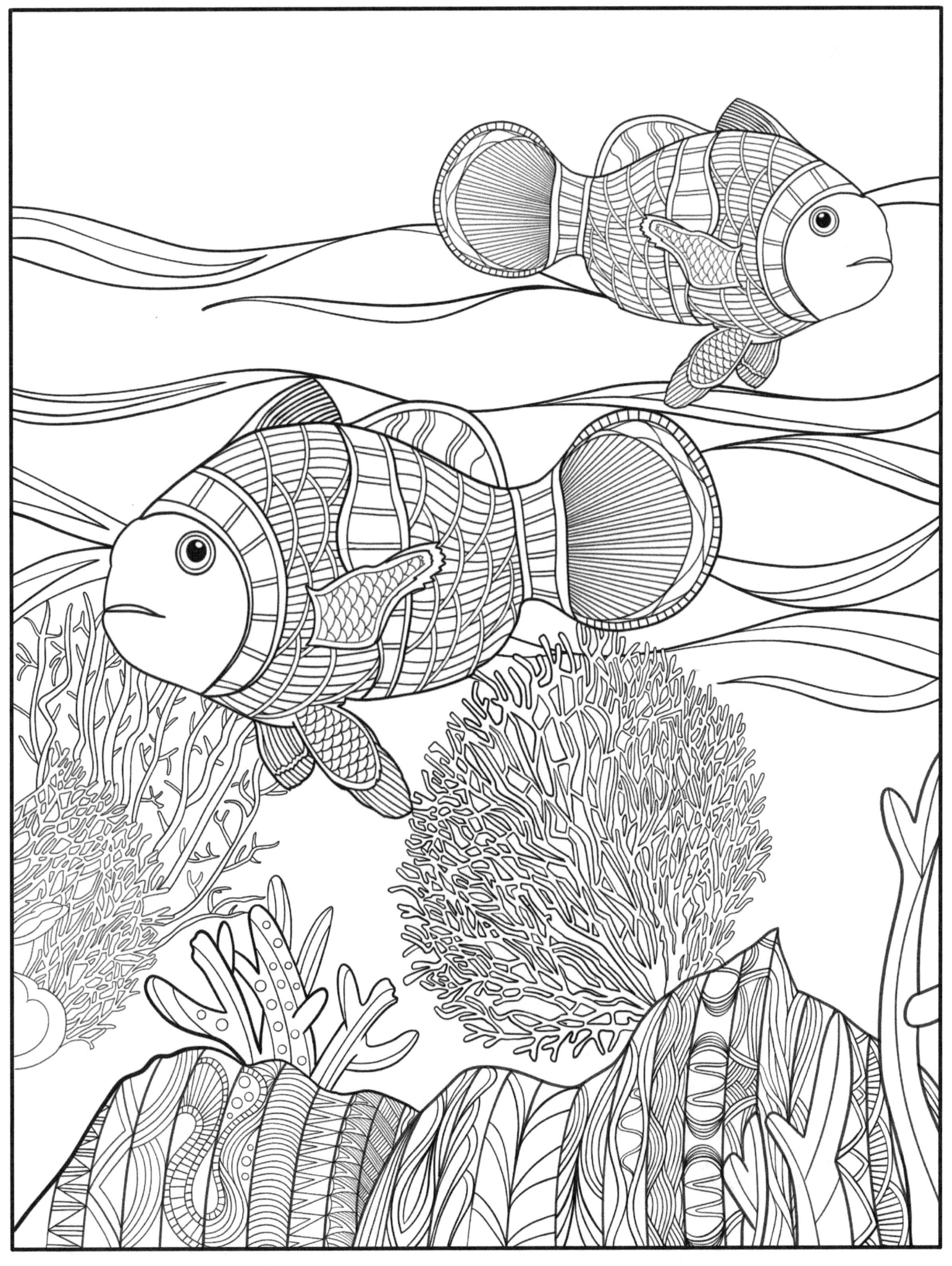

Coral Bay
Clown Fish

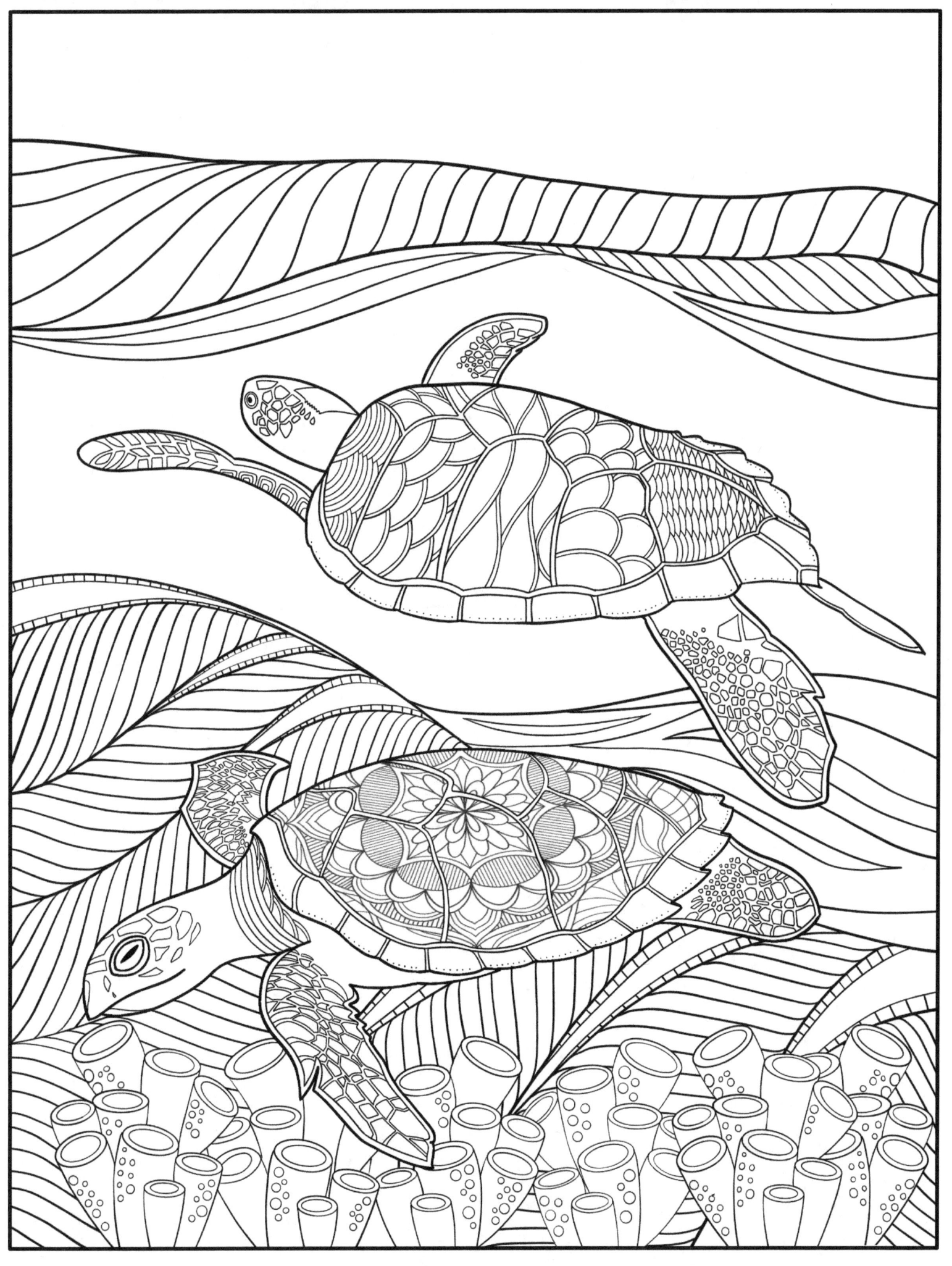

Coral Bay Turtle

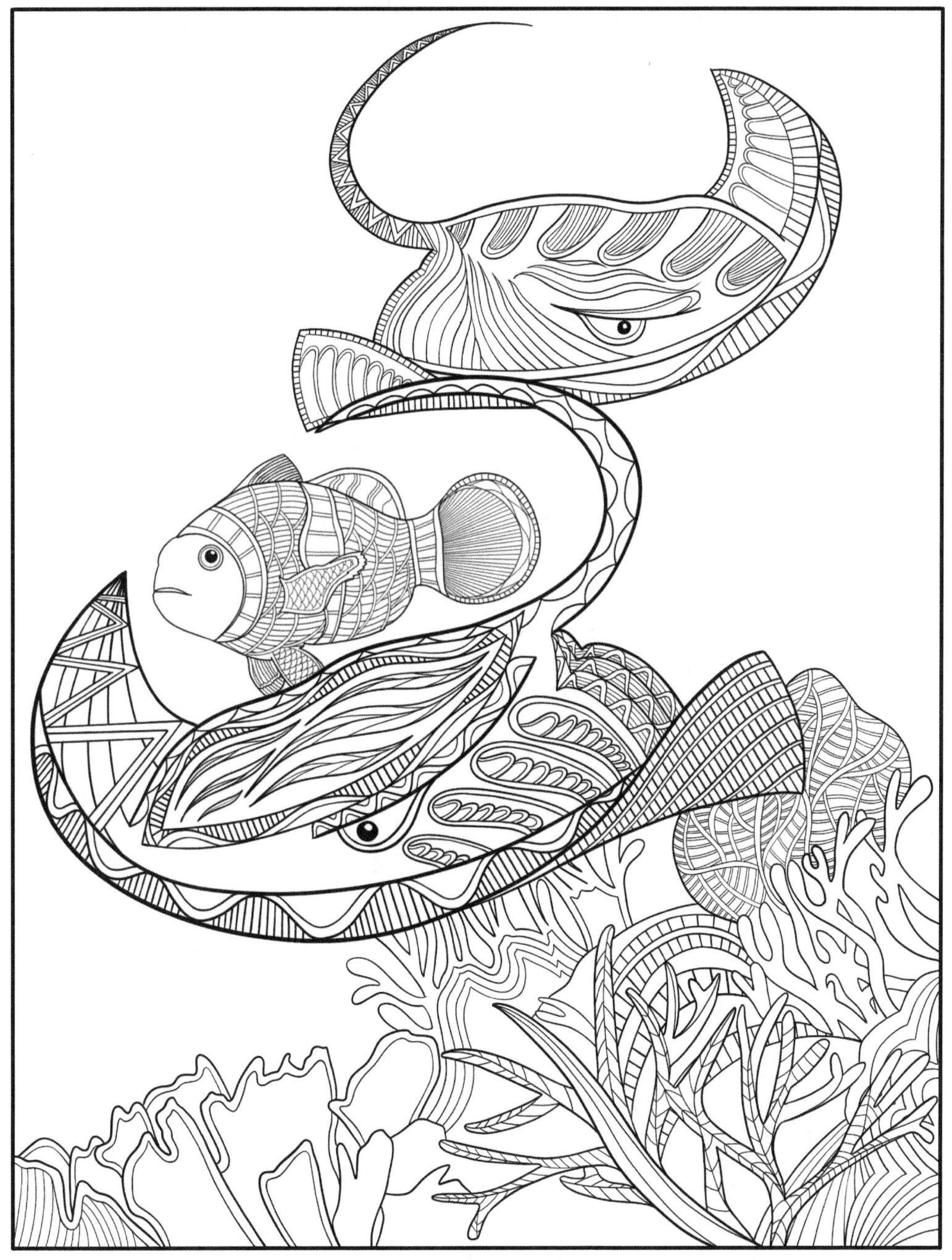

Coral Bay
Sting Ray

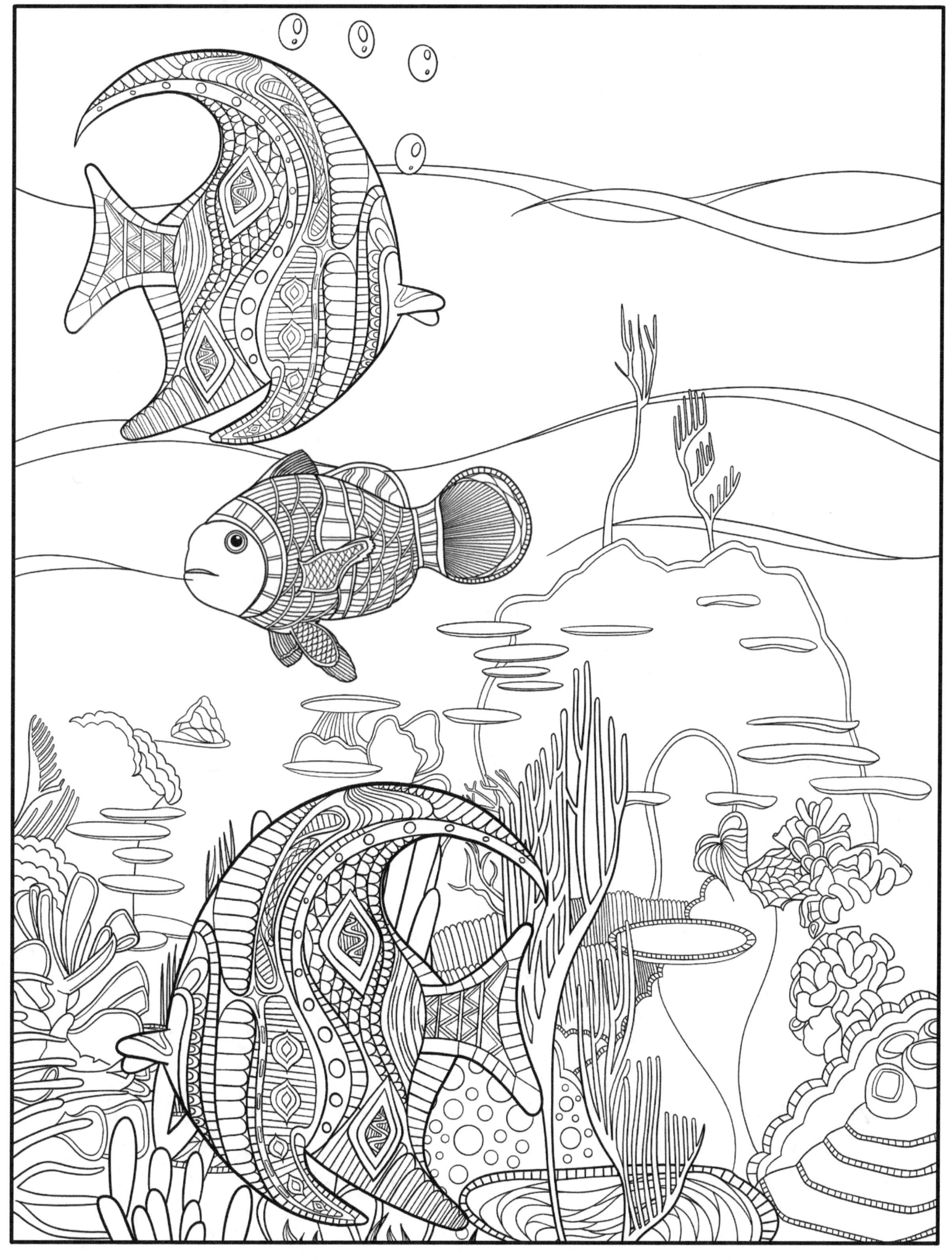

Coral Bay

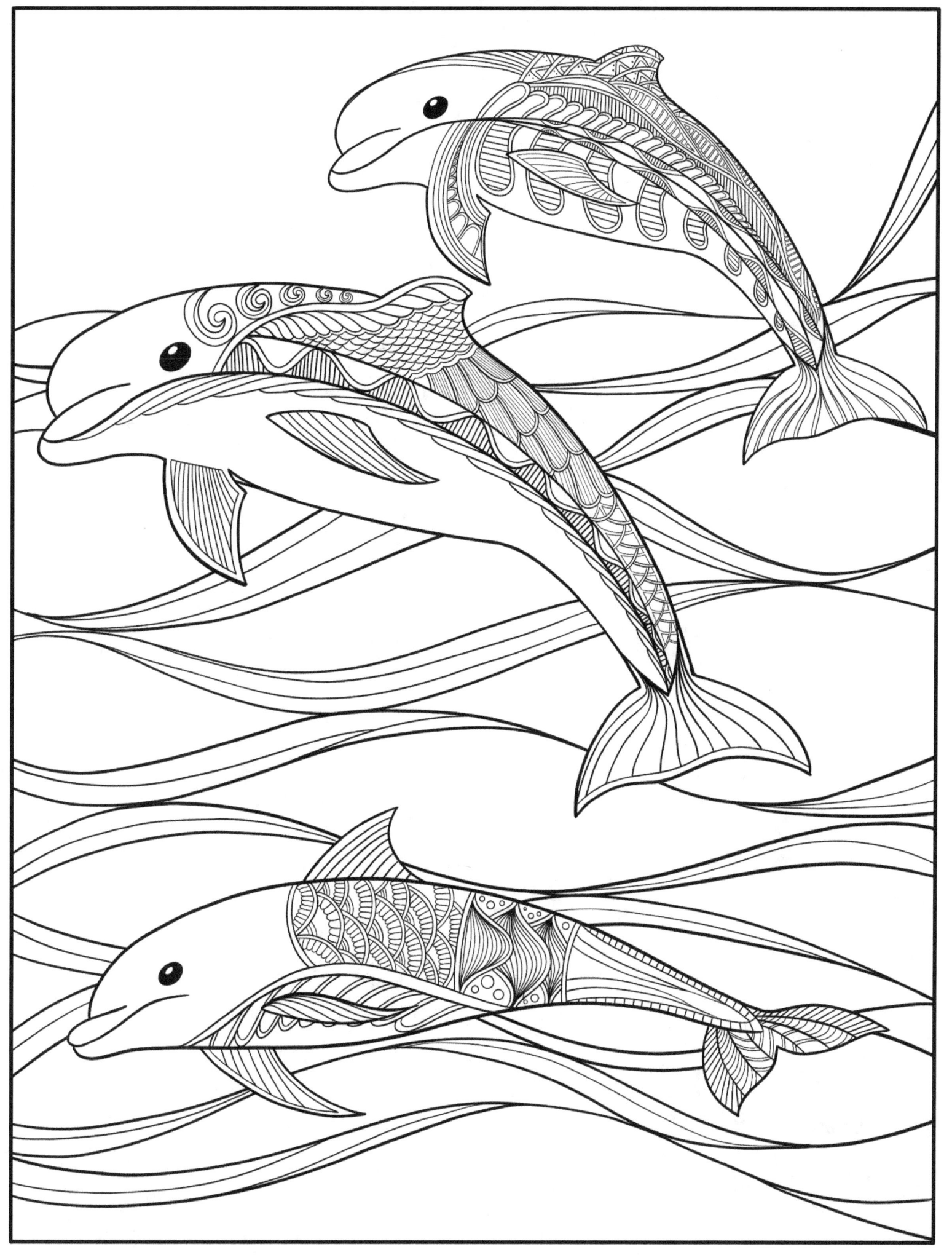

Sea Dolphins

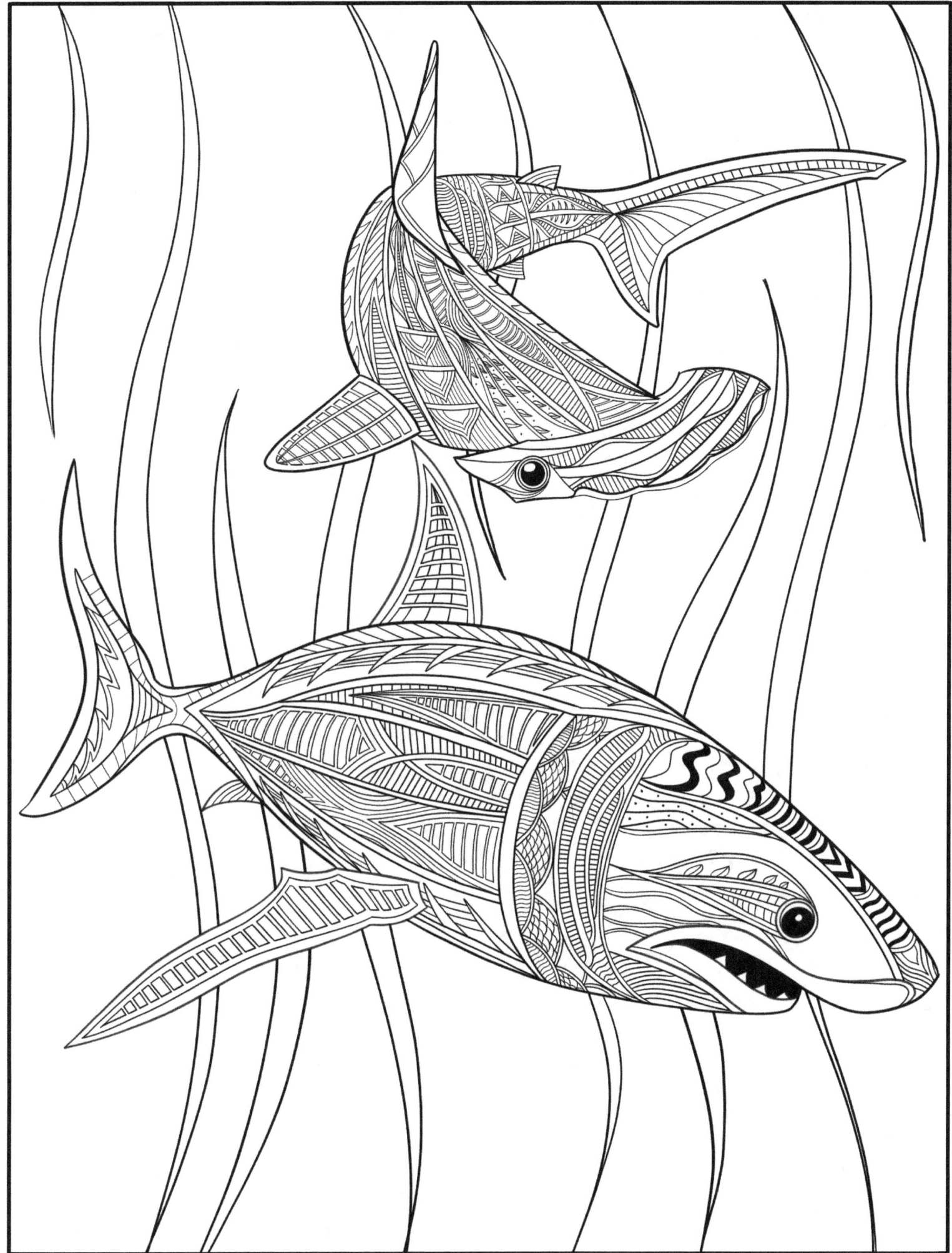

Sea
Shark

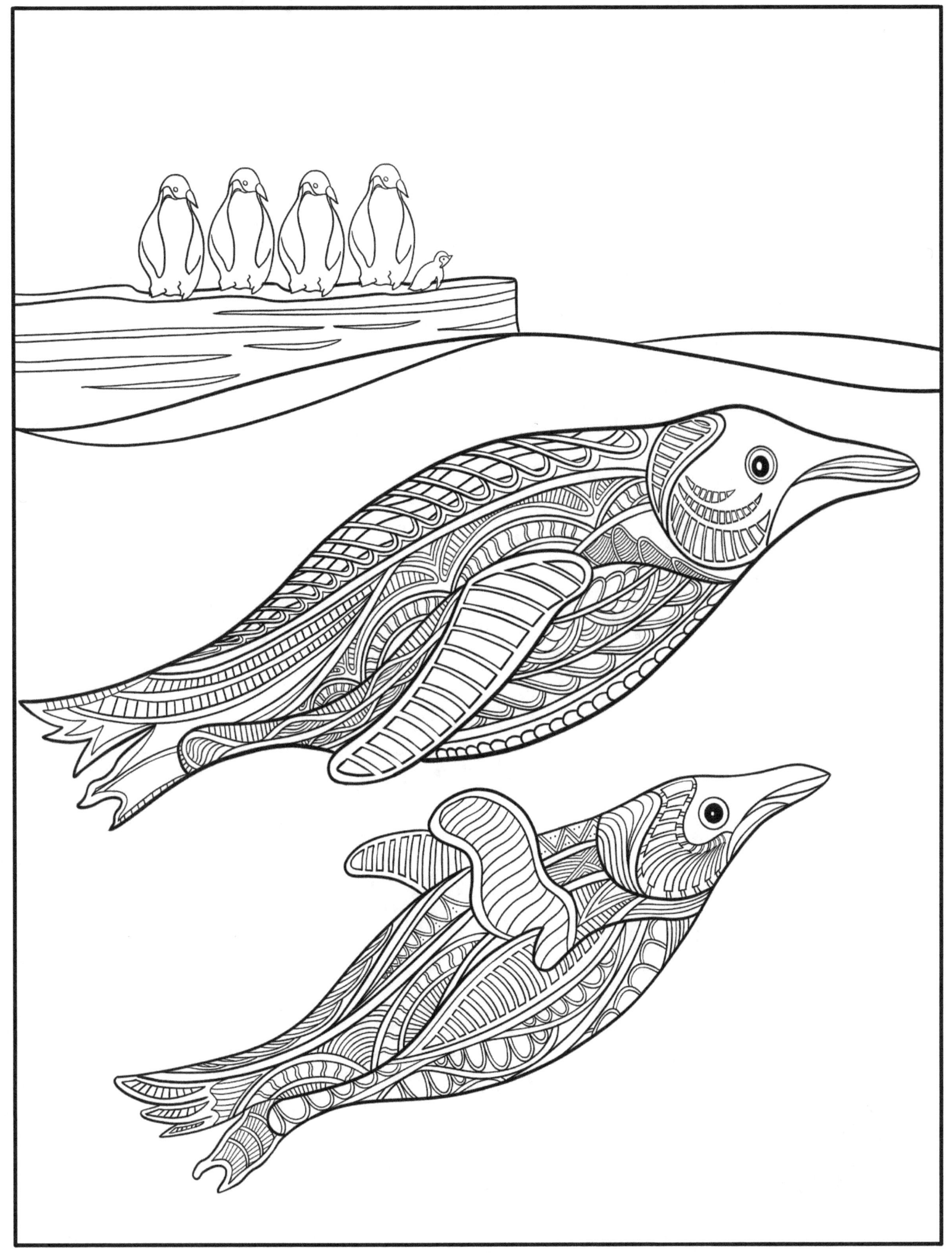

Sea Penguins

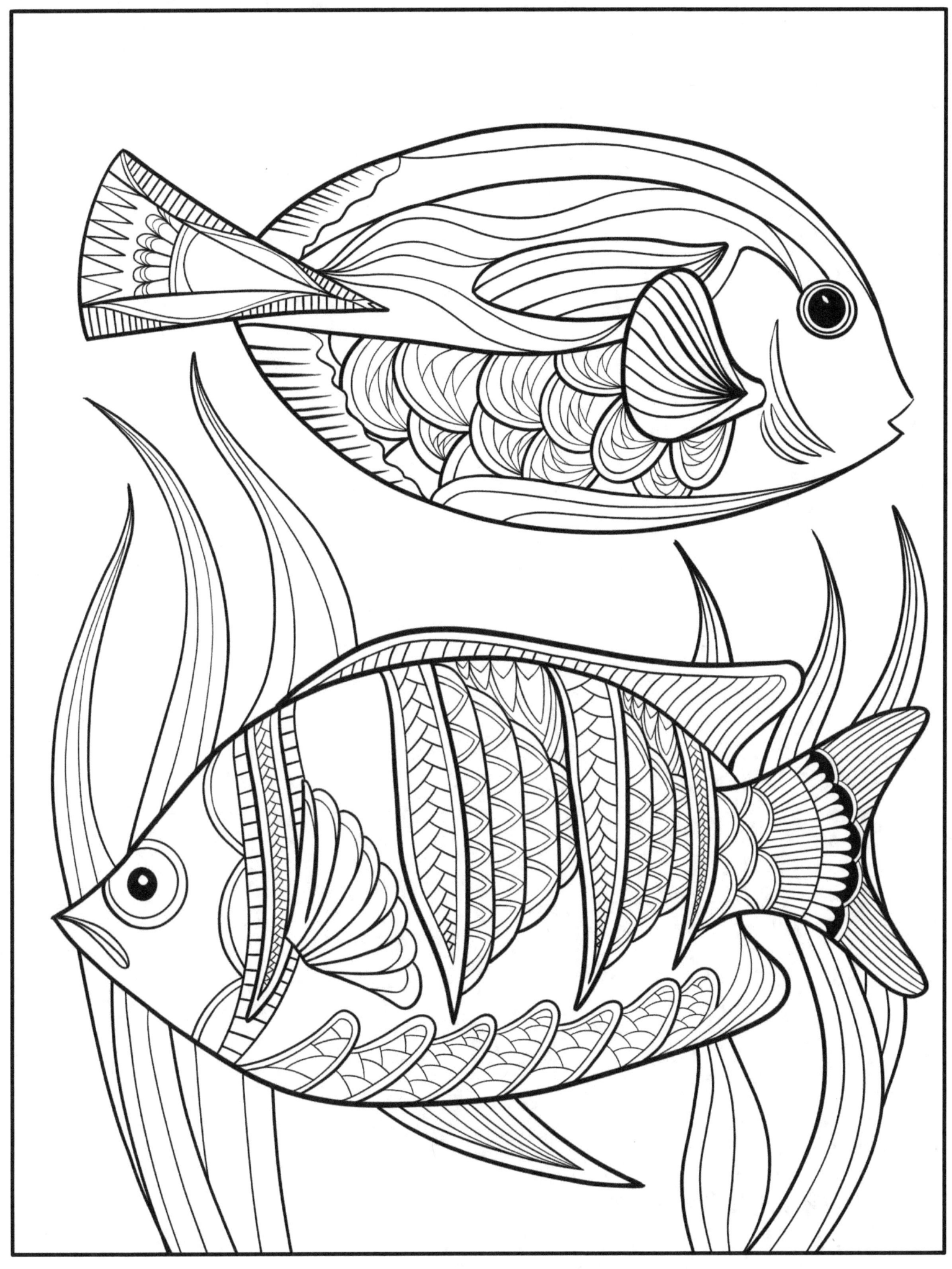

Sea
Royal Blue Tang

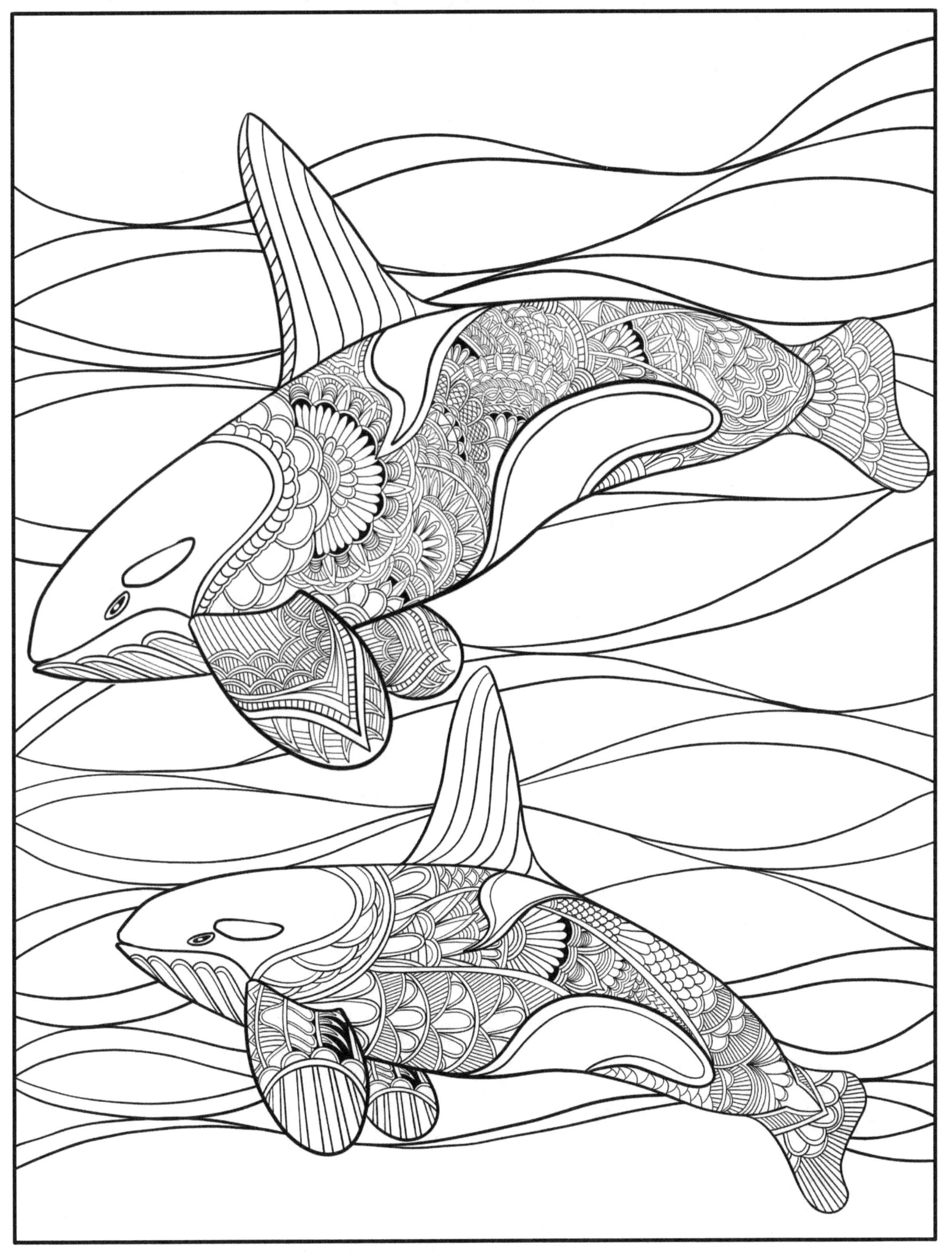

Ocean Whale

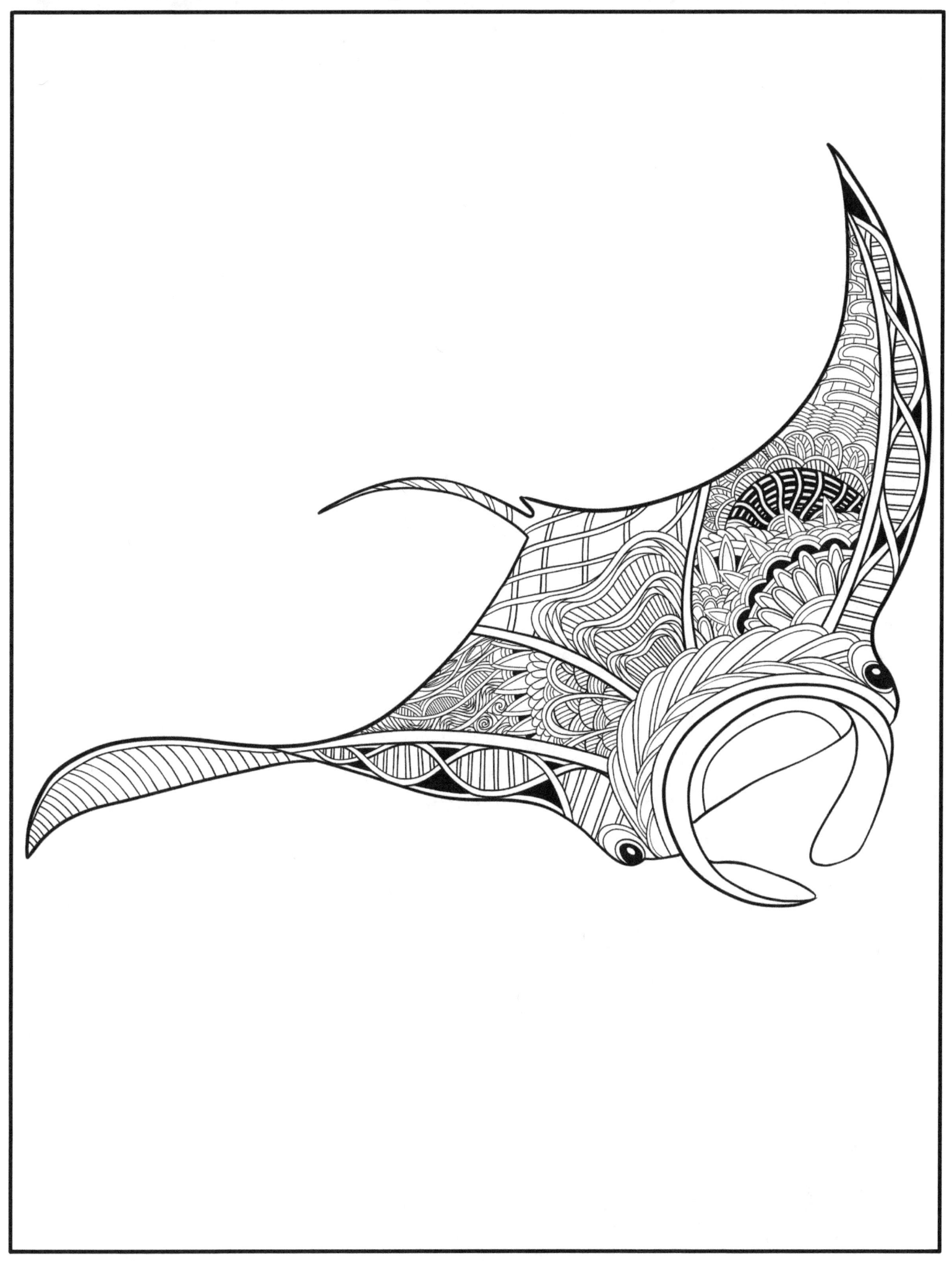

*Ocean
Manta Ray*

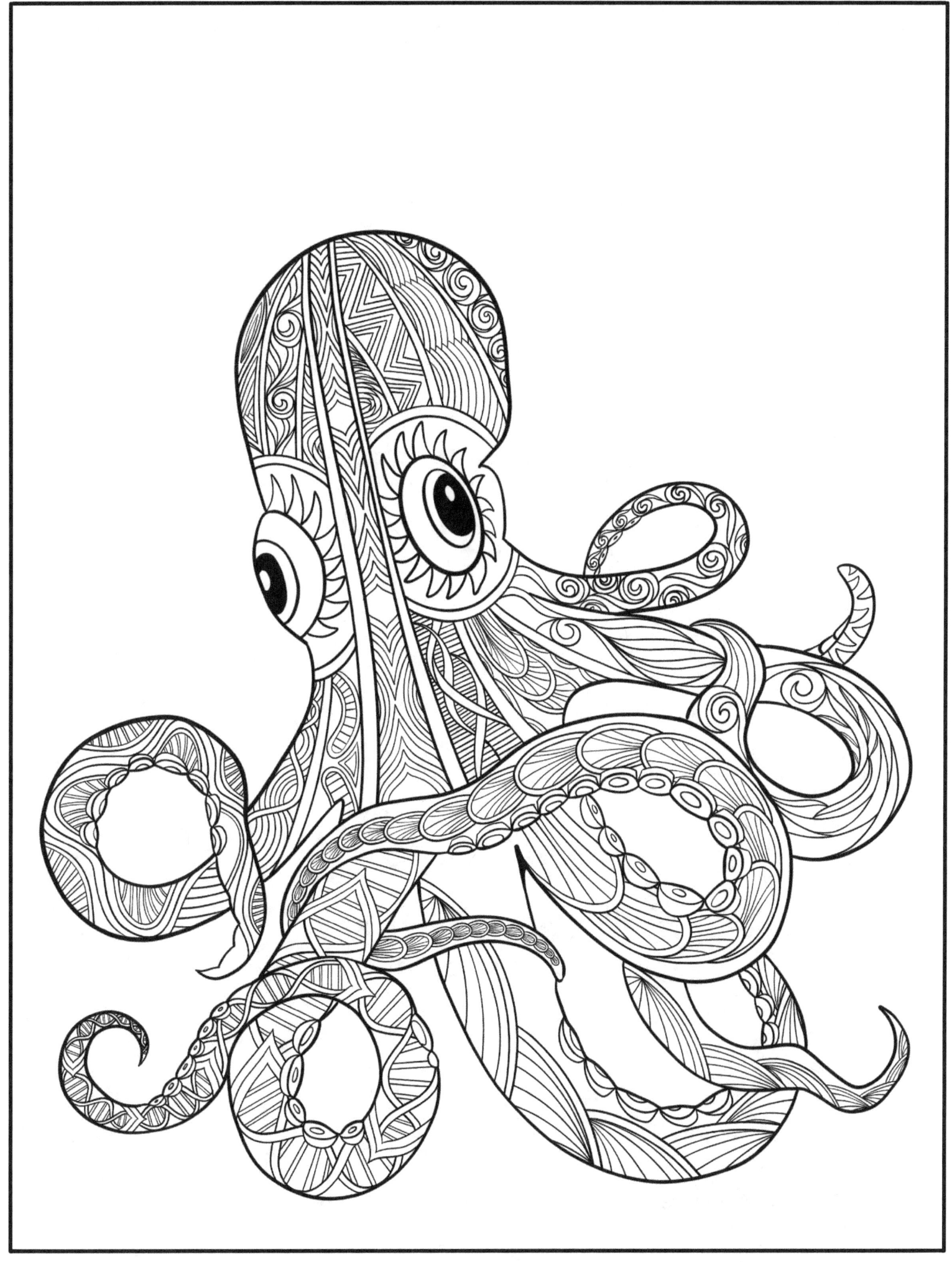

Ocean
Giant Octopus

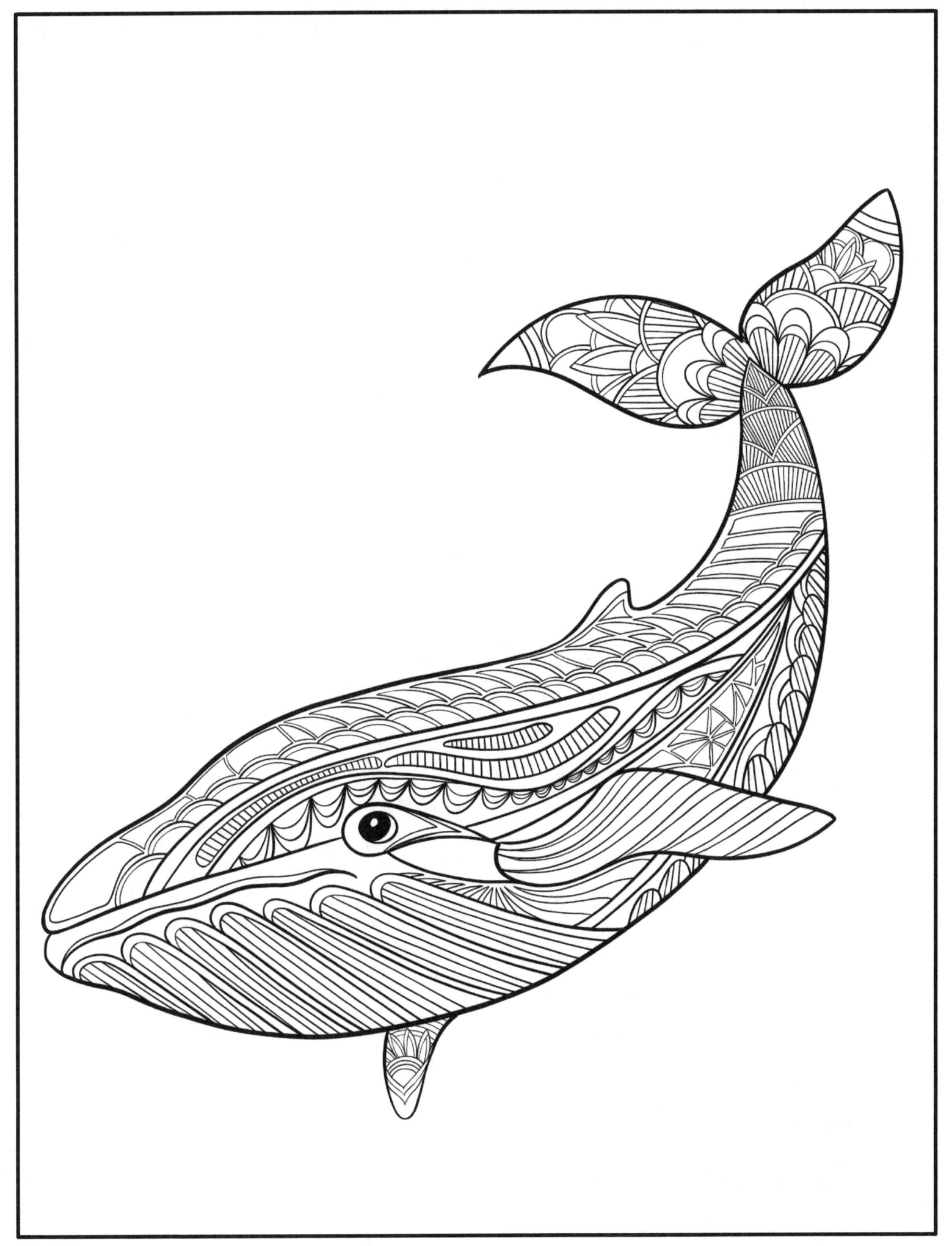

Ocean
Blue Whale

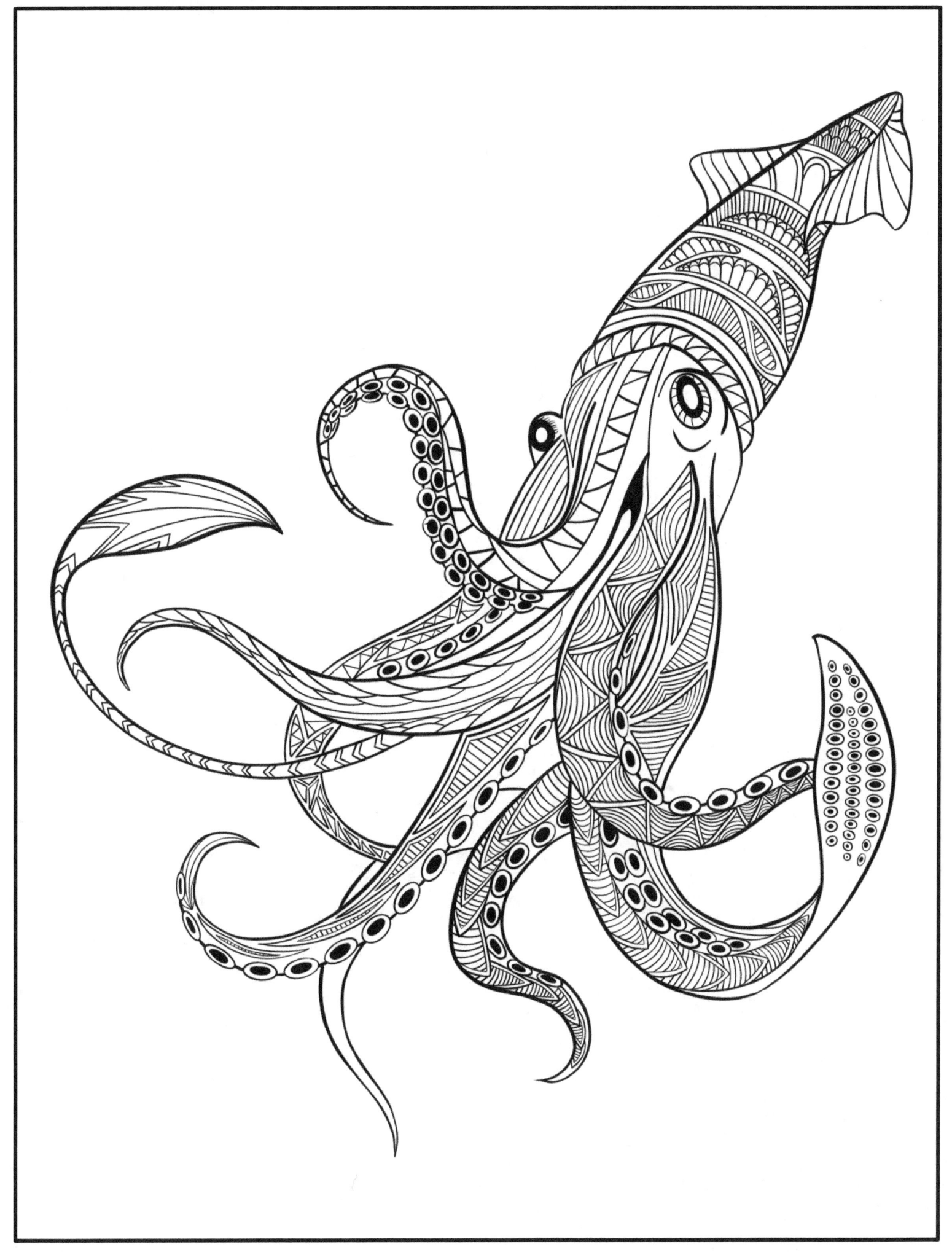

Deep Ocean
Giant Squid

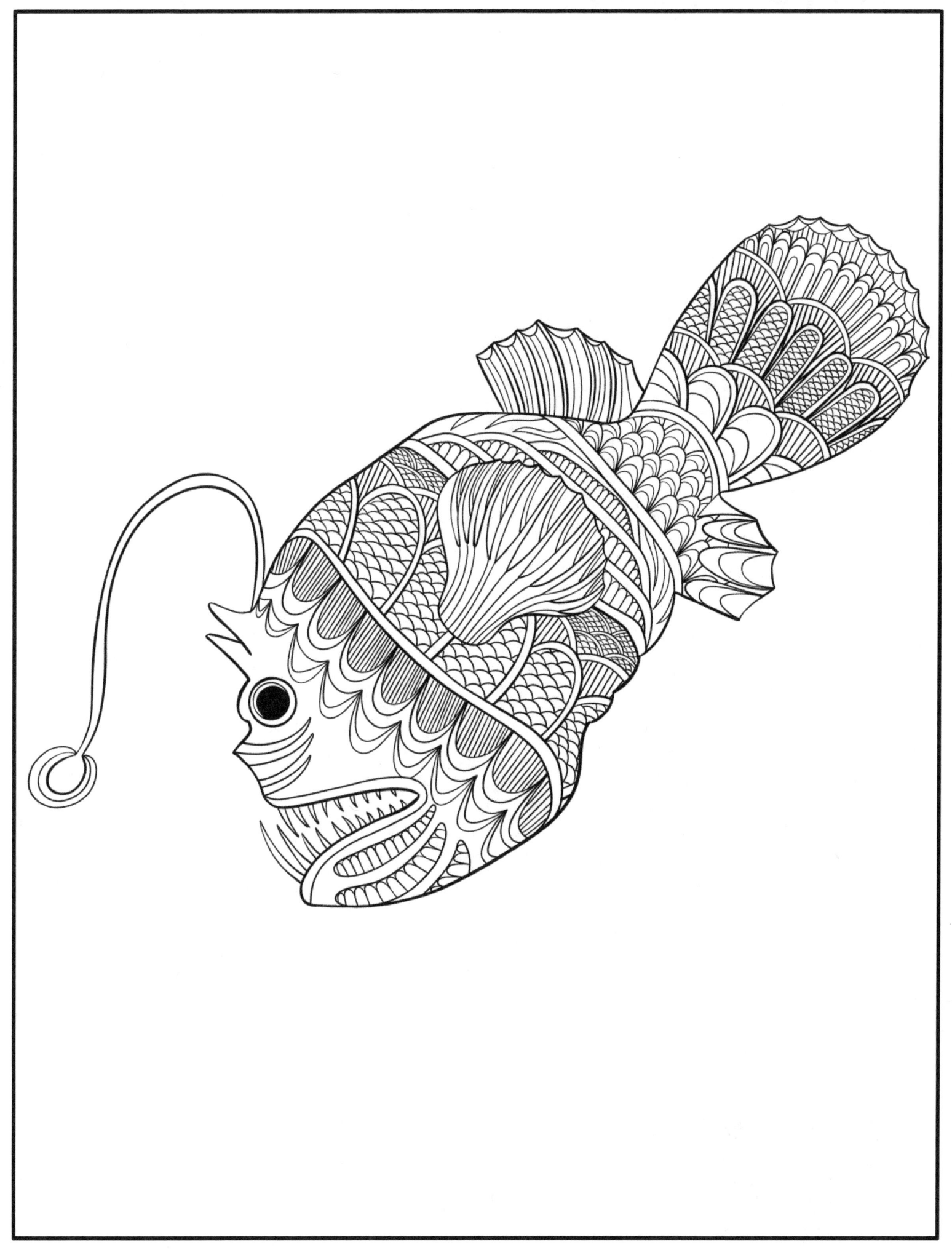

*Deep Ocean
Angler Fish*

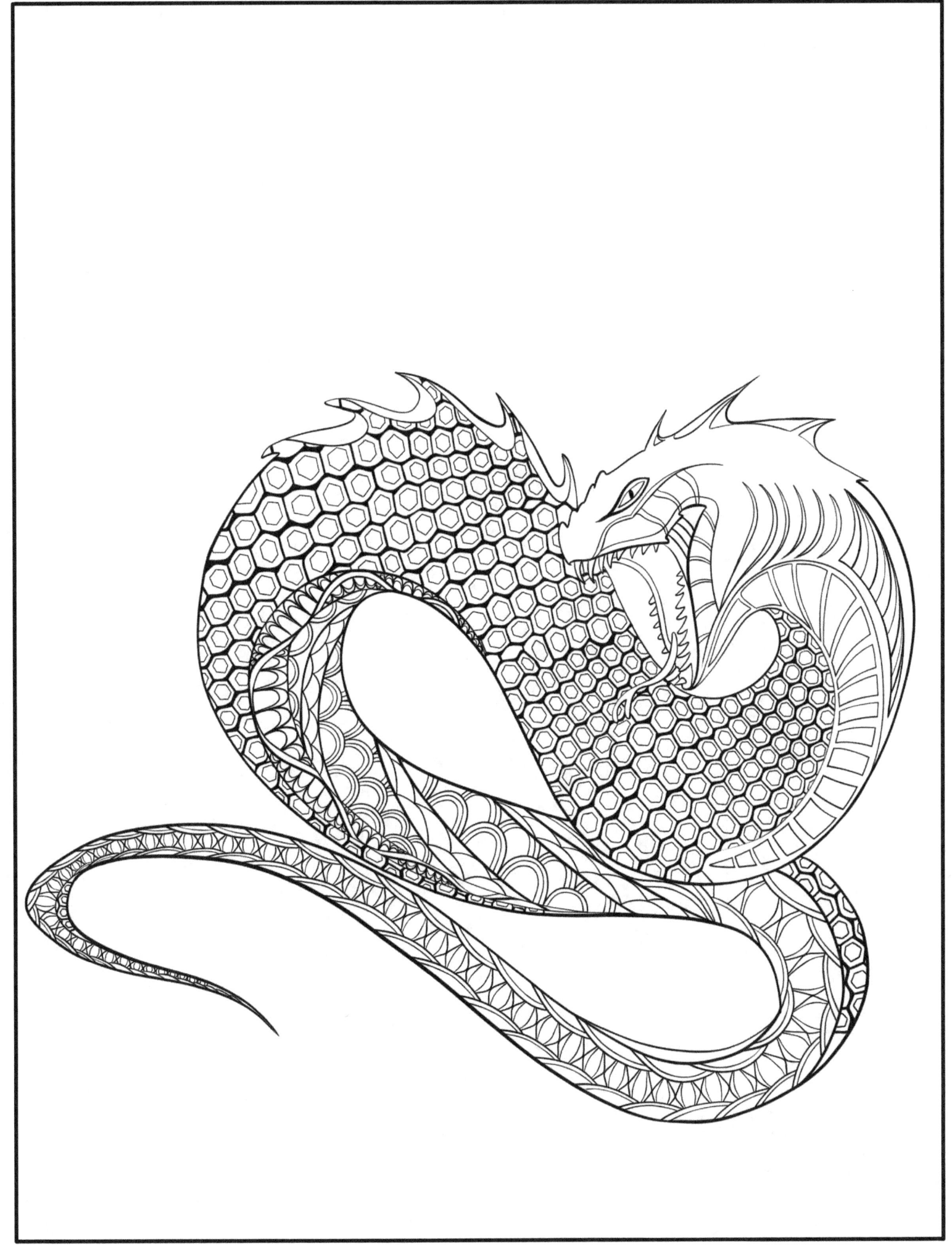

Deep Ocean
Serpent

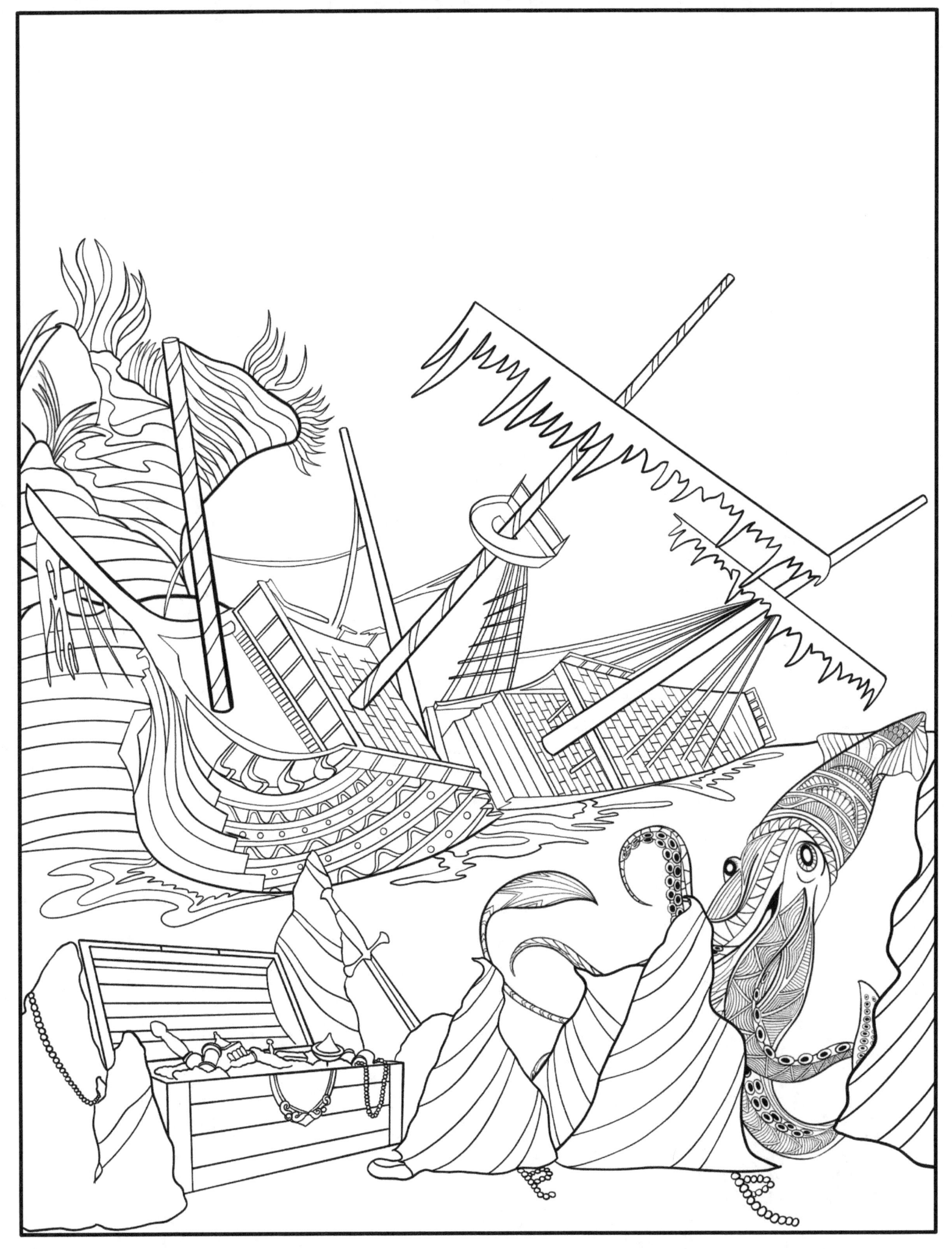

Deep Ocean Ship Wreck

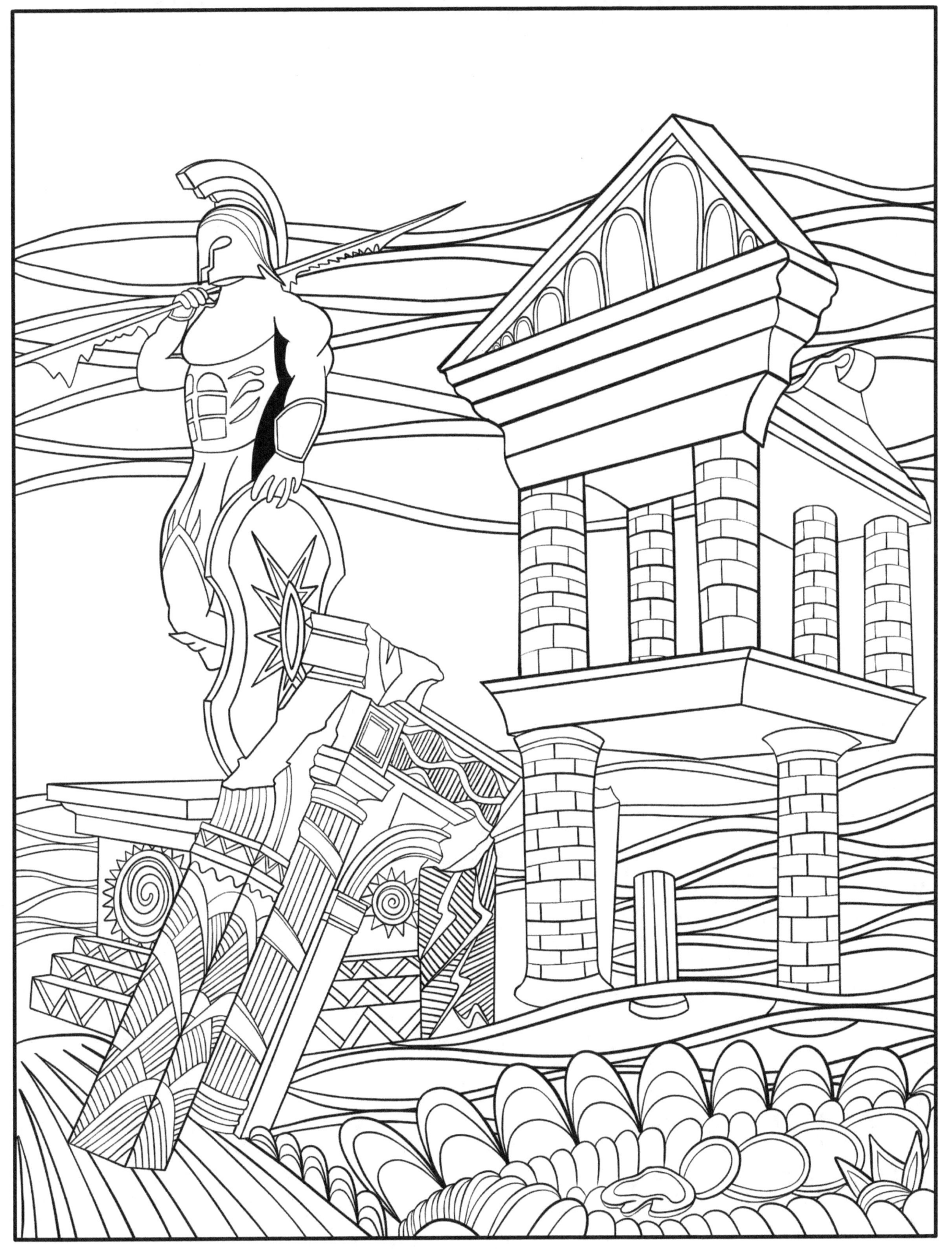

Deep Ocean
Lost Atlantis

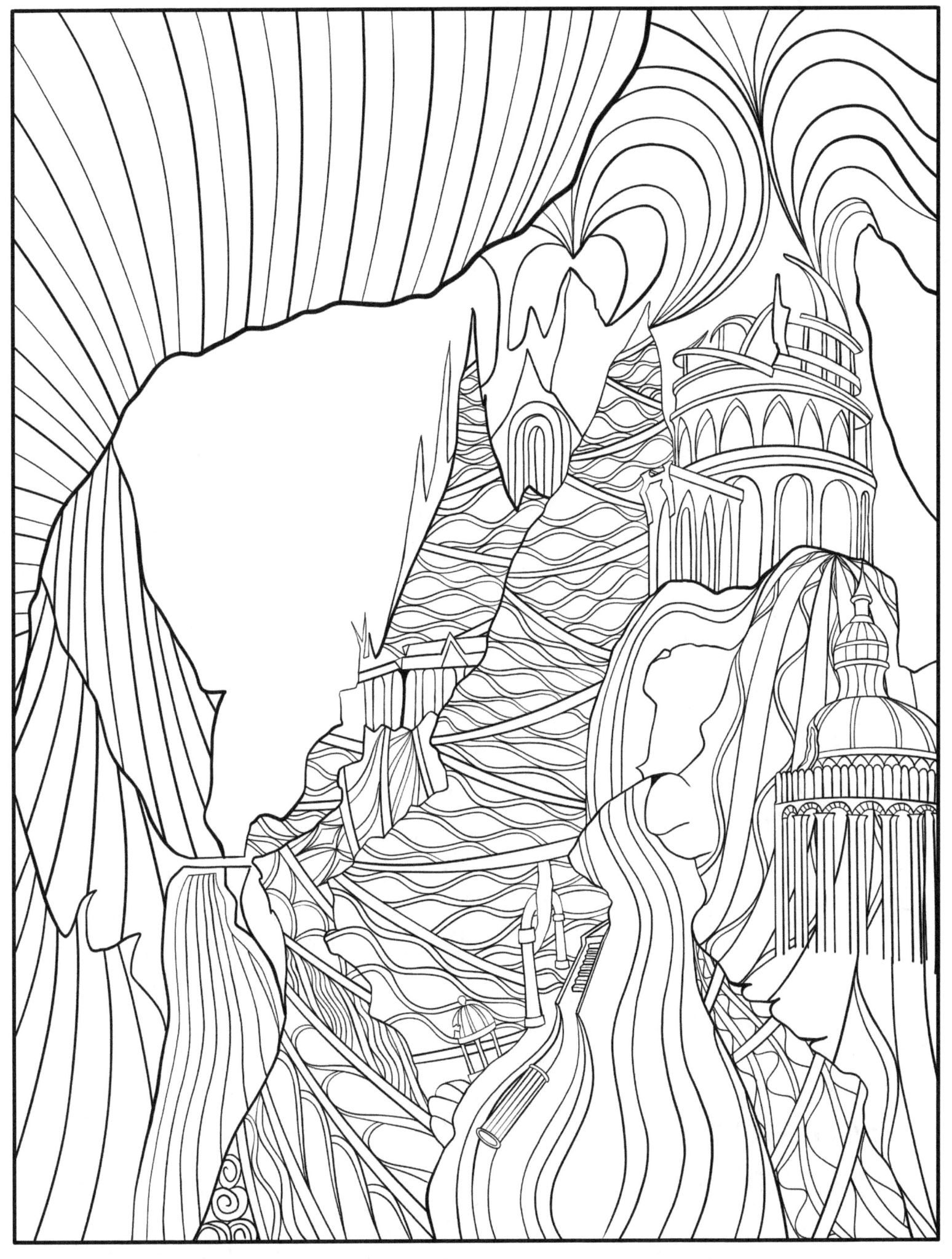

Deep Ocean
Lost Atlantis

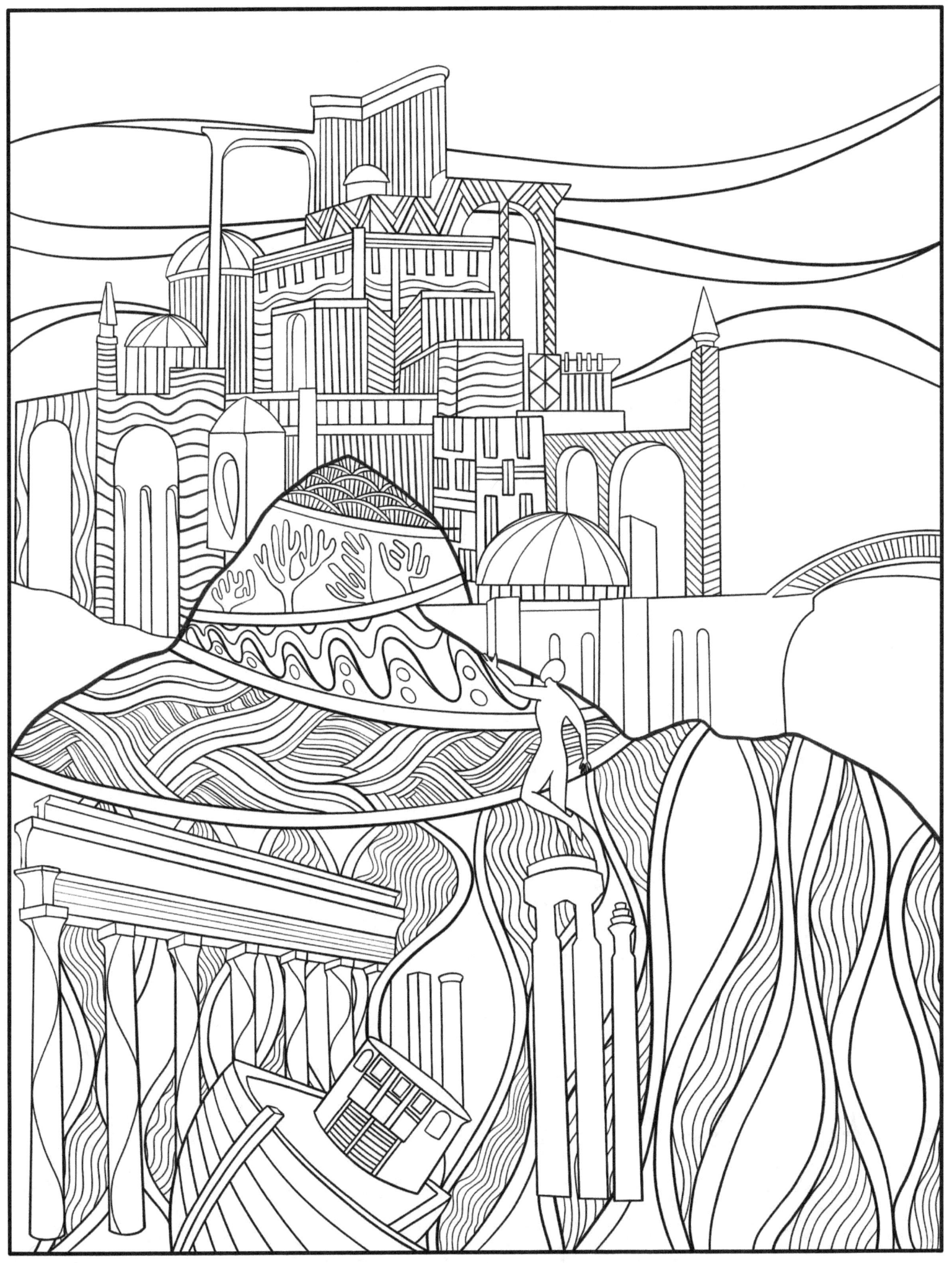

Deep Ocean
Lost Atlantis

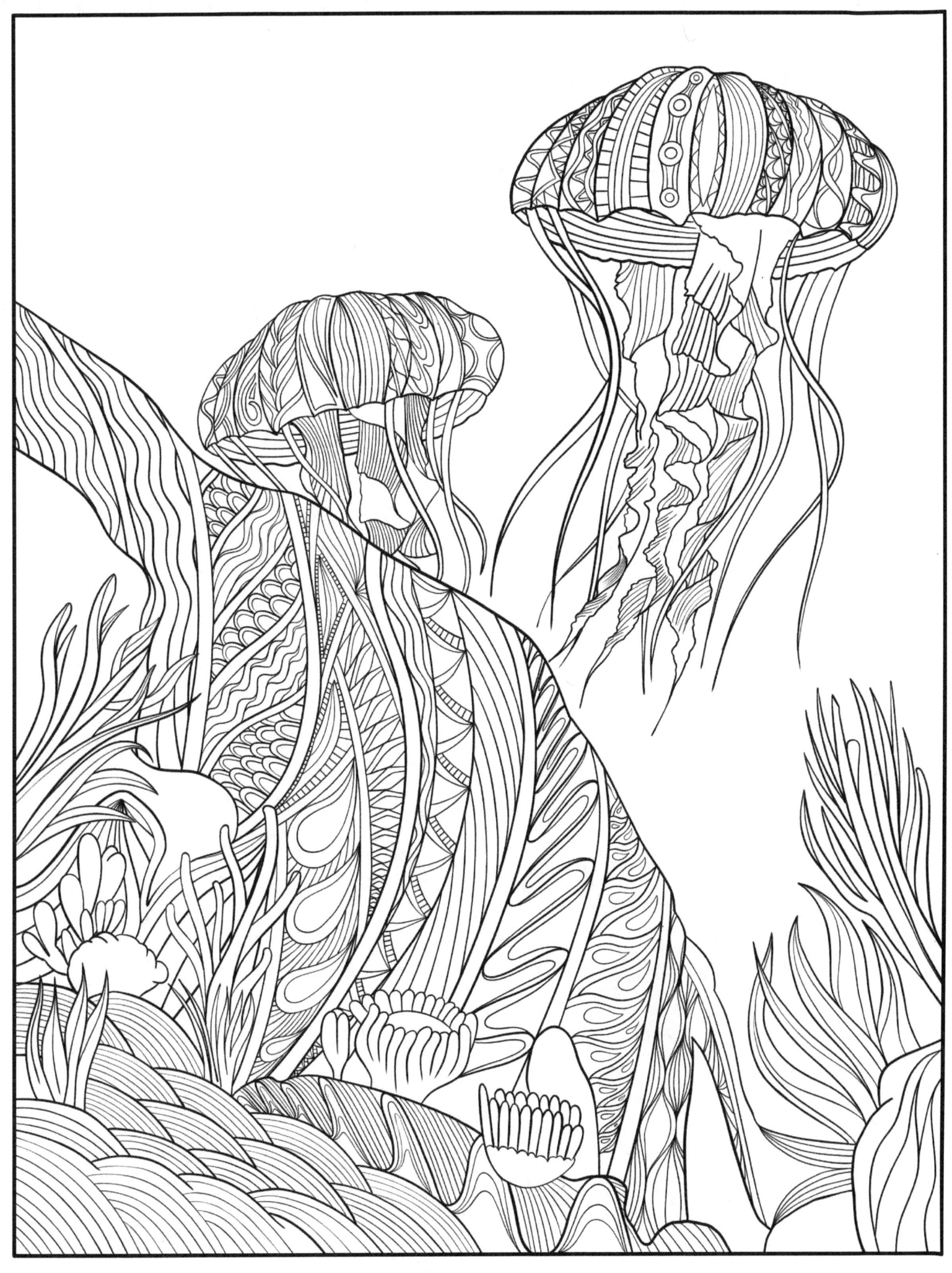

Deep Ocean
Wonders of Jelly Fish

www.ingramcontent.com/pod-product-compliance
Lightning Source LLC
Chambersburg PA
CBHW081057240526
45465CB00025B/2528